# The Procrastination Instinct

*The Wired Reason You Do Everything Except the One Thing That Matters*

Jordan Ellis

First edition, 2026

Published by Jordan Ellis

# Contents

# Foreword

I didn't set out to write a book about procrastination. I set out to figure out why I could plan a task down to the hour, believe every word of the plan, and then spend that exact hour reorganizing a drawer instead.

That's the specific stake I have in this. Not a dramatic story — a quieter, more common one. A stretch of years where the gap between what I intended to do on a given morning and what I actually did by that evening kept widening, no matter how good the intentions got. More planning didn't close it. A better calendar didn't either. What finally helped wasn't a new system. It was realizing the person avoiding the task wasn't lazy, and wasn't badly organized — she was managing a feeling, in real time, faster than I could catch her doing it.

That distinction is the whole reason this book exists. Most advice about getting things done assumes the problem is logistical: not enough structure, not enough discipline, not enough hours in the day. That assumption is wrong more often than it's right. The actual mechanism sitting underneath most procrastination has almost nothing to do with time management. It has to do with a specific negative feeling attached to a specific task, and a mind that is very, very good at finding you a way out of feeling it, right now, at the cost of a much bigger problem later.

I wrote this book for the version of you that already knows the task matters and still can't make yourself start it. You're not undisciplined. You're running a mechanism that was never built to weigh "small relief now" against "large cost in six weeks" — and nobody ever told you the fight wasn't fair.

This is a field guide, not a confession and not a cure — a map of a pattern nearly everyone carries, written by someone who spent a long time calling herself lazy before learning what was actually happening underneath. If any of the chapters ahead land closer to home than expected, you're not broken. You're just finally looking at the mechanism instead of the story you'd been telling yourself about your own character.

That's the whole reason I sat down to write this.

— Jordan Ellis

# Introduction — The Task and the Feeling

There is a task sitting somewhere on your list right now that you have not started, that you know matters, and that you are almost certainly not going to start today either.

You've told yourself several stories about why. You're too busy. You work better closer to the deadline. You're waiting for the right block of focus time. Some of that might even be a little true. But underneath the stories, if you're honest, there's usually something simpler and less flattering: starting that particular task makes you feel something you don't want to feel — a flicker of anxiety, a flare of self-doubt, a low hum of boredom, a fear that you'll sit down and discover you can't do it as well as it needs to be done — and putting it off makes that feeling go away, for now.

That's the whole book, stated as plainly as it can be stated in one sentence: **procrastination is not a failure of time management — it's an act of emotional regulation, and the task you're avoiding is rarely the real target. The feeling attached to it is.**

Say that sentence over to yourself once more, because everything that follows in this book is really just an extended, evidence-based unpacking of it, chapter by chapter, pattern by pattern: procrastination is not a failure of time management, it is an act of emotional regulation, and the task is rarely the real target. If you take nothing else from these opening pages, take that. It reframes a problem most people have spent years quietly blaming on their own character into something much more precise, much more solvable, and considerably less personal than it has probably felt.

This runs against almost everything you've been told about getting things done. The productivity industry sells you calendars, apps, and systems built on the assumption that if you just organized your time better, the avoidance would stop. Some of that machinery genuinely helps at the margins. None of it touches the actual mechanism, because the actual mechanism was never about time in the first place. You don't have a scheduling problem. You have a **pattern** problem — a small number of predictable, wired-in moves your mind makes whenever a task carries a negative feeling, the same way it flinches from a hot surface. You can't delete the flinch. But once you can see it clearly, in the half-second before it runs, you can build something that catches it before it decides for you.

Here's what that half-second actually looks like from the inside, because it's worth slowing down on before the rest of the book takes it for granted. You think about the task. Something in you registers, almost instantly, that doing it will not feel good — not painful, usually, just unpleasant in some specific, familiar way: hard, boring, uncertain, exposing. In the same instant, some other, easier action presents itself, unbidden — check the phone, tidy the desk, answer a smaller email, look something up that feels productive-adjacent. You take the easier action. The bad feeling drops, immediately and noticeably. You feel, for a moment, like you've solved something. You haven't solved anything. You've just traded a small amount of present-tense relief for a task that is now, structurally, a little bit harder to do than it was five minutes ago, because it's had five more minutes to grow a reputation in your head as the thing you're avoiding.

This book maps eight versions of that trade, each with its own specific shape, its own specific trigger, and its own specific override. Some of them will feel obvious once you see them named — you'll recognize the freeze that shows up whenever a task has to be perfect, or the private myth that you do your best work under deadline pressure, when a closer look usually tells a different story. Others are quieter and easier to miss, because they don't look like avoidance from the outside at all — a mind that keeps itself extremely busy with everything except the one task that matters, or a person who genuinely cannot start the thing and has spent years being told, wrongly, that this is a discipline problem rather than a capacity one.

Each chapter does four things. It opens with a moment you'll recognize — a composite, not any single real person, but true to how this actually looks in an ordinary life. It tells you honestly what's actually happening underneath, grounded in real, established research, without mysticism or exaggeration. It names what the pattern costs you, made concrete enough to feel. And then it gives you the overrides — specific, structural moves designed to get you started before the avoidance mechanism has time to run its usual play.

You don't need to master all eight. Most people find that one or two of these patterns are doing almost all of the damage in their specific life, and fixing just those changes the whole picture.

There's a specific kind of reader this book is not for, and naming that upfront will save both of us time: if your actual problem is that you genuinely don't know what needs to be done — a real absence of information or planning, rather than a task you know perfectly well and simply can't make yourself start — this isn't the book that fixes that. There are good books about planning and prioritization, and this isn't one of them. What follows assumes you already know, with real clarity, what the task is. The problem this book addresses sits entirely downstream of that knowing.

One more thing before we start, because it will save you some frustration later: you will likely recognize yourself in more than one of these chapters, and that isn't a sign you're unusually avoidant. It's a sign you're a normal mind, wired the way minds are wired, operating on a task list that keeps handing it things that provoke exactly the feelings it was built to escape. Naming eight patterns isn't handing you eight new problems. It's giving you eight specific, nameable handles on what has probably always felt, from the inside, like one vague, undifferentiated sense of being someone who can't seem to get to the important things.

A note on what this book is not: it's not a time-management system, and it contains no advice about money, budgeting, or finances of any kind — that's a different subject entirely, for a different book. This one is about the mind that decides, moment to moment, which tasks get done and which get quietly deferred, and the feelings that are actually running that decision underneath the surface story you tell about it.

It's worth saying something else plainly here, because it will change how you read everything that follows: this book does not treat procrastination as a single, uniform thing that one clever trick can dissolve. If it were that simple, one of the thousands of existing productivity books would already have solved it, and you wouldn't be holding this one. What actually happens, for almost everyone, is that a handful of distinct mechanisms are running underneath the single word "procrastination," each one triggered by a different kind of task, each one producing the same outward symptom — the thing not getting done — while requiring an entirely different fix underneath. The chapters ahead are organized around that insight. Each one isolates a single mechanism, shows you exactly how it works, and gives you an override built specifically for it, rather than a generic tool asked to do a job it was never actually built for.

You might also notice, reading through the coming chapters, that some of the patterns feel like they're describing the same underlying feeling from slightly different angles. That's not an accident, and it's not sloppy organization — it reflects something true about how this actually works in a real life. The dread that shows up before a task carrying real personal stakes and the dread that shows up before a task that's simply vague and unstructured can feel similar in the moment, even though the fix for one won't touch the other. Part of what this book is training you to do, chapter by chapter, is to slow down at the moment of avoidance long enough to ask which specific flavor of resistance you're actually feeling, rather than reaching for whatever generic willpower move happens to be closest at hand.

It's worth pausing on one more thing before the chapters begin, because it will shape how useful this book actually turns out to be for you: the goal here was never to produce a life with zero avoided tasks in it. That goal isn't realistic, and chasing it would be its own kind of exhausting overcorrection, trading one unhealthy relationship with your task list for another. The goal is narrower and more achievable — to notice, specifically and reliably, when the pattern running underneath an avoided task is costing you something that actually matters, and to have a real, tested tool ready when it is. Some avoided tasks genuinely don't matter enough to deserve the effort of an override, and this book will help you tell the difference, not just hand you eight new things to feel obligated about.

Let's go meet the first pattern. You've felt it more times than you could count.

# Chapter 1 — The Machine You Didn't Install

## Why willpower was never going to be enough

The chipped Formica countertop felt cold under Amelia's elbows. It was 2:47 PM on a Tuesday, and she'd been staring at the same email draft for forty-three minutes. Not *writing* the email, just...orbiting it. A small red notification pulsed in the corner of her screen, mocking her.

She glanced at the half-empty mug beside her keyboard, lukewarm coffee staining its ceramic interior like a faded watercolor. She *should* finish this email. Completion would unlock a small sense of relief, clear one item off her to-do list, and potentially prevent another nudge from David, her manager—a man who communicated almost exclusively through passive-aggressive Slack messages. But right now, staring into the digital abyss of that unfinished message felt...unpleasant. A low hum of anxiety vibrated in her chest.

It wasn't fear, exactly.

More like a vague sense of inadequacy, mixed with the weight of expectation. Like she was perpetually on the verge of disappointing someone, and this email was just another opportunity to fall short.

And then, almost automatically, her gaze drifted to Instagram. Not to connect with anyone, not for any specific purpose. Just to scroll. To absorb the curated lives of strangers, a brightly lit distraction from the grayness of her own unfinished task. A photo of someone's perfectly plated avocado toast flashed across the screen – a vibrant green against bleached wood. Then a travel influencer posing in front of a turquoise ocean, impossibly tanned and carefree. Each image was a tiny escape hatch, a momentary reprieve from the feeling she couldn't quite name but desperately wanted to avoid.

She knew, on some level, that this was ridiculous. That scrolling through social media wasn't solving anything. It was simply trading one discomfort for another – replacing the low-grade anxiety of an unfinished task with the subtle, insidious envy of other people's highlight reels. But the impulse was too strong to resist. The machine had taken over. A little gremlin in her brain, expertly rerouting attention towards whatever offered the quickest path to emotional neutrality, regardless of the long-term consequences.

I've watched this exact pattern play out hundreds of times—in clients, in friends, in myself on particularly bad Thursdays when a looming deadline sits there like a ticking bomb and I find myself suddenly, urgently convinced that reorganizing my desk drawer is the most important thing I could possibly be doing right now. And every single time, the script is identical: the task triggers discomfort, the discomfort triggers escape, the escape produces temporary relief followed by compounding dread. It's so predictable it's almost boring. Except it's not boring when it's your life getting quietly derailed, week after week, by a mechanism you never agreed to install.

Somewhere along the way—and it wasn't a conscious decision, more like a slow accumulation of learned responses—you were handed a piece of machinery you never asked for. It came fully assembled, tuned to a specific job: get you away from bad feelings, fast, by whatever route is quickest. And it's been quietly running a portion of your task list ever since, not because you're lazy or lack discipline, but because the machine was built for a different problem than the one it's currently being asked to solve.

It operates beneath awareness. A silent autopilot hijacking your intentions before they even fully form.

This isn't about willpower. Everyone talks about willpower like it's some kind of muscle you can strengthen through sheer force of repetition, but that's treating the symptom, not the cause. It's about understanding that machinery. About recognizing that procrastination isn't a moral failing, a personality flaw, or a sign of deep-seated dysfunction. It's a deeply ingrained biological response – an ancient survival mechanism misfiring in the modern world.

And to keep fighting it with sheer force of will is like trying to push a river upstream. Exhausting. Ineffective. Ultimately futile.

You'll feel good for about ten minutes after forcing yourself through something unpleasant, but the underlying pattern remains unchanged, waiting for its next opportunity to hijack your attention.

Picture two people, each with the same unpleasant task sitting on their list for the same three days: that difficult conversation they need to have with someone close to them, one they've been rehearsing in their head at 2 AM and avoiding in daylight. One of them feels the familiar tightness whenever the task crosses their mind, notices it, sits with it for a beat, and picks up the phone anyway, uncomfortable the entire time. The other feels the same tightness and, within the same minute, has found something else that suddenly seems urgent – a different message to answer, a small chore that's been "waiting," a scroll through something that isn't the conversation.

Same species. Same rough situation. Wildly different outputs.

And neither of them consciously chose their response the way they'd choose which shirt to wear. The response arrived pre-loaded, faster than deliberate thought could weigh in, assembled from old wiring plus a lifetime of specific reinforcement neither of them designed on purpose.

This is what the machine looks like when it runs unexamined: not one dramatic failure, but a hundred small forks in the road, each resolved before you knew there was a decision being made at all.

---

Your mind's core wiring around discomfort, threat, and effort was shaped over a period of human history in which avoiding an unpleasant feeling was frequently the *correct call.* A rustle in the grass that produced a flicker of dread was worth fleeing from, immediately, without deliberation – the cost of a false alarm was low, and the cost of ignoring a true one could be fatal. A mind built for that world developed a general-purpose rule that served it extremely well for an extremely long time: when something produces a sharp negative feeling, move away from it, fast, and figure out the details later if you survive long enough to need them.

It wasn't about being *smart*. It was about being alive.

None of that was irrational. It was, in fact, very well calibrated to the conditions it evolved under. A mind that lingered to reason through every source of unease before acting on it was a mind whose owner was, on balance, less likely to make it to the next generation than one that flinched first and reasoned second. Examined on its own terms, the avoidance instinct is a reasonable, even elegant, solution to a real and recurring problem.

The machine isn't broken.

It's running in an environment it was never built for.

And that mismatch—that perfectly functional system responding to entirely non-threatening stimuli—is where everything falls apart.

Here's what changed, and how fast it changed, measured against how long the machine had to adapt to the old conditions: modern task lists are made almost entirely of a category of discomfort the machine has no good instinct for – a slow-building, low-grade unease attached to a task that poses no physical danger at all, that can be deferred indefinitely with no immediate consequence, and whose real cost only shows up much later, compounded, disguised as a deadline crisis, a damaged relationship, or a body of work that never got made.

There was no equivalent of "the unstarted report" or "the unanswered difficult email" in the environment that built your avoidance reflex. The reflex has no calibration for a threat that isn't actually a threat to your survival, only to some abstract future version of your life you can't fully feel yet.

This is a genuine mismatch, and it's worth being precise about what kind. It isn't a mismatch between a good machine and a bad one. It's a mismatch between a well-built machine and a world it was never calibrated for. The same wiring that made your ancestors flinch from a real, immediate danger is the wiring that makes you flinch from opening a document that might reveal you're not as capable as you'd like to believe – except the document can't actually hurt you, and flinching from it, this time, doesn't remove the danger.

It just delays the moment you'll have to face it, usually with less time and more stakes attached.

---

Trace a single moment all the way through and the mismatch stops being abstract.

You sit down to start the task. Something in you registers discomfort before you've done anything at all – not because the task is dangerous, but because some part of it resembles a category the machine has learned to treat as threatening: possible judgment, possible failure, possible confirmation that you're not enough. The machine reads this the way it would read a genuine threat, and it reaches for the same tool it's always reached for: get away from the feeling, now.

It has no separate setting for "this feeling is data about a task, not a warning about your survival." It only has the one setting, tuned over a very long time to treat sharp discomfort as something to escape rather than something to sit inside of for the twenty minutes it would actually take to get started.

And here's a layer that makes this more personal than "humans dislike discomfort in general": the machine doesn't just run the species-wide default. It gets fine-tuned, over your specific lifetime, by whatever happened to be reinforced along the way.

If a specific category of task was repeatedly followed, in your own history, by criticism, disappointment, or a feeling of falling short – a creative project shown to someone who was unkind about it, a difficult conversation that went badly the one time you tried it, a performance evaluated harshly at a formative moment – your machine doesn't just inherit the general human dislike of discomfort. It inherits a specific, personal flag on that exact category of task, and that flag will quietly determine which of the patterns we'll explore together hits you hardest, years before you can name why a particular kind of task makes your stomach drop while a similarly difficult one doesn't touch you at all.

Think about Maya Angelou for a second. One of the most celebrated writers of the twentieth century, author of *I Know Why the Caged Bird Sings*, recipient of more than fifty honorary degrees. And yet—and this is documented in multiple interviews—she wrote most of her books in hotel rooms because she couldn't write at home. She'd rent a room with nothing but a bed, a table, two chairs, and some legal pads. She'd arrive at 6:30 in the morning with a bottle of sherry, a deck of cards to play solitaire, Roget's Thesaurus, and the Bible. She'd write until early afternoon, then go home and edit what she'd written.

Why the hotel room? Because at home, there were too many escape routes. Too many ways for the machine to redirect her attention when the work got difficult or when self-doubt crept in. The hotel room wasn't about finding inspiration—it was about eliminating the easy exits her avoidance mechanism would otherwise exploit. She was engineering around the machinery, creating a structural barrier between herself and the reflexive escape.

And even then, even with all those precautions, she'd still spend chunks of time playing solitaire. The machine still ran. It just had fewer places to run *to*.

You might be thinking: "But Maya Angelou was a world-class writer dealing with the weight of telling profound, painful truths about race and trauma in America. I'm just trying to answer an email or finish a spreadsheet. It's not the same thing."

And you're right—it's not the same thing. Except it is, in the one way that matters here: the mechanism producing the avoidance is identical. The machine doesn't care about the objective importance of the task. It only cares about the *feeling* the task produces. An email that might reveal you don't have the answer your boss expects can trigger the same avoidance response as a memoir chapter that might expose your deepest wounds. Different content, same machinery.

The machine responds to emotional threat, not rational threat. And that's why fighting it with rationality—telling yourself the task isn't actually that hard, reminding yourself of the consequences of not doing it, making lists and schedules—almost never works for more than a day or two.

---

It's worth walking through a few concrete versions of this mismatch, because the shape it takes changes depending on what kind of discomfort the task is producing.

Sometimes the discomfort is the fear of being judged and found wanting – a creative piece, a proposal, an application, anything where the outcome will say something about your ability. Sometimes it's the low hum of boredom a task produces, with no fear attached at all, just a flat unwillingness to spend attention on something that promises no stimulation in return. Sometimes it's the ambiguity of not knowing where to start, which produces a formless kind of resistance that's easy to mistake for laziness because it doesn't come with any identifiable fear attached to point to.

This explains why two people facing the same objective task can have wildly different reactions to it. One person opens a blank document to start a piece of creative work and feels mild, manageable resistance. Another opens the same kind of blank document and feels something closer to dread, because somewhere in that person's history, a blank page once led somewhere painful, and the machine remembers the category long after the conscious mind has stopped thinking about the original event.

I saw this play out with Sarah, a graphic designer I worked with years ago on a book cover. Sarah was brilliant—a real eye for color and composition, the kind of artist who could make a mundane subject sing. But she had this…loop. She'd accept a project, become intensely enthusiastic about it initially, then slowly descend into a state of anxious paralysis as the deadline approached.

It wasn't that she lacked talent or skill. It was that her internal process seemed to actively sabotage itself right when momentum should have been building.

I remember one particularly frustrating week where we were nearing the final revisions on the cover. Each email exchange started with her apologizing for the lack of progress, followed by a detailed explanation of everything *else* she'd managed to accomplish – reorganizing her digital files, researching new software, even deep-cleaning her home office. Useful tasks, absolutely, but none of them moving the actual project forward.

She wasn't lazy. She was exquisitely good at creating the illusion of productivity while avoiding the one thing that felt genuinely terrifying: letting someone see her work in progress.

I asked Sarah what specifically made staring at the cover so difficult. It wasn't the technical challenge, she insisted. We were sitting in a coffee shop near her studio—she'd picked the meeting place, probably as another micro-avoidance of actually working in the space where the unfinished cover sat waiting on her monitor.

"It's just…the judgment," she said finally, swirling the ice in her water glass. "The fear it won't be good enough. That I'll put something out there and everyone will see how much of a fraud I am."

She hadn't voiced this aloud to anyone, not even her husband. It was just…there, humming beneath everything she did. And the moment that feeling surfaced—the tightness in her chest, the little voice whispering doubts—her brain immediately started scanning for an escape route. Not a productive one, but an *emotional* one. A way to make the discomfort stop, even if it meant delaying the inevitable and piling on more stress later.

She didn't consciously choose to reorganize files. She felt *compelled* to do so, as if her hand were guided by something other than rational thought.

That compulsion, that subtle redirection of energy—that was the machine at work. Not a malicious force, just an ancient system misfiring in a modern context. A system built to protect Sarah from genuine threats – physical danger, social rejection – now responding to the entirely harmless threat of constructive criticism on a book cover.

The feeling wasn't the problem. It was what she *did* with the feeling that created the cycle of procrastination.

---

Think back for a moment to those ancestors of ours, scanning the savanna for predators. A rustle in the grass didn't require analysis—it demanded an immediate response: freeze or flee. There wasn't time to weigh the probabilities, assess the risks, or consider long-term consequences. Survival depended on acting instinctively, prioritizing safety above all else.

That instinct is still baked into our brains, even though most of us now face threats that are far more abstract—a looming deadline, a difficult conversation, a fear of failure. The machine hasn't changed;

the environment has. And it's responding to these modern "threats" with the same urgency and single-mindedness as it would have to an actual saber-toothed tiger.

The cost of that mismatch isn't immediately obvious. It doesn't result in physical pain or immediate danger. Instead, it manifests as a slow erosion of potential—missed opportunities, unrealized goals, and a persistent sense of being stuck.

Sarah wasn't suffering from a lack of talent. She was suffering from the cumulative weight of countless small avoidances, each one adding to her stress levels and chipping away at her self-confidence. The pressure built not because the task was difficult, but because she repeatedly deferred confronting it, turning a manageable challenge into an overwhelming crisis.

Let me be specific about what that erosion looks like when you zoom out far enough to see the full cost.

Sarah's loop didn't just affect that one book cover. It affected every project she took on afterward. Each time the pattern repeated—initial enthusiasm, slow descent into paralysis, last-minute panic to deliver something—she accumulated a little more evidence that she "couldn't be trusted" to manage her own process. Her confidence didn't just take a hit; it took repeated, compounding hits. And each hit made the next project scarier, which made the avoidance kick in earlier, which made the eventual crisis more acute.

By the time we worked together, she'd turned down two major opportunities in the previous year—projects she desperately wanted, with clients who specifically sought her out—because she "didn't have the bandwidth." That was the story she told them. The story she told herself was closer to: "I can't handle the stress of disappointing someone who has high expectations of me."

The machine had trained her to avoid not just the immediate discomfort of working on a difficult task, but the entire category of tasks that might produce that discomfort. She was pre-emptively protecting herself from feelings that hadn't even happened yet. And in doing so, she was systematically shrinking the size of her professional life.

That's what the machine costs you when it runs unchecked. Not just the missed deadline or the unfinished task, but the gradual narrowing of what you're willing to attempt at all.

---

And here's where most productivity advice goes wrong: it focuses on willpower, discipline, and motivation – as if Sarah could simply *force* herself to overcome her fear and get back to work.

But willpower is a finite resource, depleted by stress and emotional exhaustion. Trying to brute-force your way through discomfort is like running a marathon with broken legs—possible, maybe, but unsustainable and ultimately self-defeating.

The machine doesn't respond to logic or reason. It responds to feelings. And the more you try to suppress those feelings, the stronger they become.

I know this because I've tried the willpower approach myself. For years. And it worked exactly as well as you'd expect: I'd have these brief, glorious bursts of productivity where I'd convince myself *this time* I'd stay on top of things, *this time* I wouldn't let tasks pile up until they became emergencies. I'd make elaborate plans, color-coded schedules, accountability systems. I'd wake up early, full of resolve.

And it would last maybe four days.

Then something would happen—a task would trigger that familiar discomfort, the machine would kick in, and I'd find myself three hours deep into reorganizing my entire filing system or reading articles about productivity instead of actually doing the work. And then I'd feel like a failure, which would trigger *more* avoidance, and the whole cycle would compound until I was buried under a pile of delayed tasks and self-recrimination.

The problem wasn't that I lacked discipline. The problem was that I was trying to override a deeply embedded biological mechanism with sheer force of will, and that's not a fight you can win through effort alone. You have to change the conditions under which the mechanism activates.

What Sarah needed wasn't more motivation. She needed a structural intervention. A way to bypass the avoidance mechanism altogether.

We started small—literally. Instead of asking her to work on the entire cover at once, we broke it down into ridiculously small steps: "Change the color of one leaf." Then, "Adjust the brightness of the title." Each task was so manageable that it barely triggered the fear response, allowing her to make incremental progress without getting bogged down in anxiety.

It wasn't about making the task *easier*. It was about changing the emotional equation. By lowering the stakes and removing the immediate threat of judgment, we created a space where Sarah could actually work—not because she suddenly found more willpower, but because the machine had less reason to panic.

You might be thinking this sounds almost insultingly simple. "Just break down tasks into smaller steps"? That's supposed to be the revolutionary insight?

And yeah, I get it. It sounds like basic time management advice you'd find in a listicle titled "7 Productivity Hacks That Will Change Your Life!" But that reaction—that dismissiveness—is actually part of the problem. Because it misses the point entirely.

This isn't about efficiency. It's about emotional regulation.

It's about recognizing that procrastination isn't a problem of *how* you work, but of *why* you avoid working in the first place. And the 'why' is almost always rooted in an attempt to manage discomfort, not a lack of planning or organization.

The tiny steps worked for Sarah not because they were a clever productivity trick, but because they created a pathway for her to start moving before the machine's threat-detection system fully activated. The machine looks for big, scary, judgeable outcomes. A task framed as "design a professional book cover that will be seen by thousands of people" trips every alarm. A task framed as "change the color of one leaf" doesn't even register as a potential threat.

Same work. Different framing. Completely different emotional response.

Within three weeks, Sarah had finished that cover—and more importantly, she'd started to see the pattern herself. She began recognizing the moment when her brain started scanning for escape routes, and she got better at intervening before the avoidance took hold. Not by fighting it, but by designing around it.

---

I see this pattern everywhere, once you know what to look for. Take Mark, a novelist I advised last year who was stuck on the third chapter of his new book—a scene involving a difficult confrontation between two characters. He'd been staring at the same paragraph for weeks, endlessly revising it, deleting and rewriting, convinced he couldn't get it right.

It wasn't writer's block, not exactly. Mark knew what needed to happen in the scene; he just couldn't bring himself to *write* it.

Why?

Because the confrontation mirrored a painful argument he'd had with his own brother years ago—an unresolved conflict that still haunted him. Every time he tried to write the dialogue, he felt a surge of anxiety, a familiar ache in his chest. The scene wasn't just about fictional characters anymore; it was about revisiting his own emotional wounds.

And so, like Sarah with her book cover, Mark's machine kicked in—not by making him unable to write, but by making him obsess over the *details* of writing: font choices, paragraph breaks, even the color of the cursor on the screen. Anything to avoid confronting the actual content of the scene.

Mark wasn't avoiding work. He was avoiding feeling.

He wasn't lacking discipline. He lacked a mechanism for safely processing difficult emotions.

And that's true for most of us. We tell ourselves we're procrastinating because we're lazy or unmotivated, but the reality is far more complex—and far more human.

Consider what happened when Mark finally acknowledged this connection. I asked him to write the scene badly on purpose—to give himself explicit permission to make it terrible, melodramatic, unrealistic. "Write it like a soap opera," I told him. "Make the characters yell ridiculous things. Make it over-the-top."

He looked at me like I'd suggested he burn his manuscript.

But he tried it. And something shifted. Because when the goal was to write it *badly*, the machine had nothing to protect him from. There was no threat of judgment when the whole point was to produce garbage. He wrote three pages in one sitting—awful, overwrought dialogue that made him cringe. But buried in those three pages was the core emotional beat he'd been circling for weeks. Once he had that on the page, even in its terrible first form, he could shape it into something real.

The breakthrough wasn't about finding the right words. It was about removing the conditions under which avoidance felt necessary.

---

Here's what I want you to understand: the problem isn't your lack of willpower. It's that you've built a system—or rather, inherited a system—where avoiding discomfort feels safer than confronting it. You've reinforced the machine every time you chose the easy path: scrolling through social media instead of writing, cleaning your office instead of making a difficult phone call, starting another task rather than finishing the one that matters most.

And the more you reinforce that pattern, the stronger it becomes. Not because you're weak, but because the brain is exquisitely good at learning which behaviors reduce discomfort in the short term, even when they increase it in the long term.

The machine doesn't care about your long-term goals. It cares about *right now*. And right now, avoiding the thing that makes you anxious feels better than doing it. Every single time you make that choice, you're teaching your brain that avoidance is the correct response to discomfort. You're deepening the groove.

Knowing that you're procrastinating is not the same as being free of it. You can read this chapter, understand precisely why an unfinished draft feels safer than a finished, judgeable one, nod along with every example—and still feel the exact same pull the next time you sit down to start something that could turn out to be not good enough.

That isn't a failure of comprehension. It's proof the mechanism is doing exactly what it was built to do, and understanding a mechanism intellectually doesn't automatically reroute it.

You don't defeat this kind of mechanism by arguing with it. You defeat it by building a specific, structural override for each specific way it produces avoidance—a small design change that gets you moving before the machine's usual escape route has time to activate.

You don't fix an old machine by arguing with it. You fix it by engineering around its limitations.

And that is precisely what we're going to do, one pattern at a time.

---

But before we get to the engineering, you need to see one more thing clearly: what the machine is *actually* trading when it routes you away from the difficult task.

It's not trading present comfort for future success, though that's how it feels in the moment. It's trading one kind of discomfort for another. The discomfort of sitting with uncertainty or fear of judgment gets swapped for the discomfort of knowing you're letting yourself down, again. The anxiety of starting gets replaced by the anxiety of not having started, which is almost always worse because it compounds.

Sarah's story didn't end with that one book cover. We stayed in touch. A few months after we finished that project, she sent me an email. She'd just turned down another opportunity—a big one, the kind that could have shifted the trajectory of her career. A well-known publisher wanted her to design a series of covers for a celebrated author's backlist. Dream project. Exactly the kind of work she'd told me she wanted.

She said no.

When I asked her why, she said, "I just couldn't handle the pressure of disappointing them."

The machine had won again. Not because she'd procrastinated on the project—she never even started it. She'd pre-emptively avoided the entire situation because her brain had learned that the safest way to avoid the discomfort of potential failure was to never put herself in a position to fail at all.

That's the real cost. Not the individual tasks you put off, but the slow, systematic shrinking of your life. The opportunities you stop seeing as opportunities and start seeing as threats. The projects you never start. The conversations you never have. The risks you never take.

The machine convinces you that you're protecting yourself. And in a narrow, immediate sense, you are. You're protecting yourself from the discomfort of being judged, of possibly failing, of discovering you're not as capable as you hoped.

But you're also protecting yourself from the only pathway to the thing you actually want.

---

Start here: tomorrow, pick one task you've been avoiding. Not the biggest or scariest one on your list—pick something medium-sized, something that's been sitting there for a few days producing that low hum of dread every time you look at it.

Before you do anything else, before you open the file or start the email or make the phone call, just notice what happens in your body when you think about doing it. Where do you feel it? Chest? Stomach? Throat? What's the quality of the feeling—sharp or dull, hot or cold, tight or heavy?

Don't try to change it. Don't argue with it. Just notice it.

Then set a timer for ten minutes and make a deal with yourself: you're going to sit with that feeling and do the task anyway, but only for ten minutes. After ten minutes, you can stop, no guilt, no judgment. The point isn't to finish the task. The point is to practice moving *toward* the discomfort instead of away from it, and to discover that the feeling doesn't actually get worse when you do—it usually gets *better*, or at least changes into something more manageable.

Most of the time, you'll keep going past the ten minutes. Not because you suddenly found motivation, but because starting was the hard part, and once you're in motion the machine has less to grab onto.

But even if you stop at ten minutes, you've done something more important than making progress on the task: you've started training a new response. You've shown your brain that the feeling isn't a warning signal that needs to be obeyed, just information that can be acknowledged and moved through.

This isn't the full solution—we're going to build much more sophisticated overrides for specific patterns in the chapters ahead. But this is the foundation everything else rests on: the recognition that the discomfort isn't the problem, and avoiding it isn't the solution.

The machine will keep running. It's been running for a very long time, and it's not going to shut off just because you've read a chapter explaining how it works.

But you can learn to see it running. And once you can see it, you can start building around it.

---

The next time you sit down to work and feel that familiar pull toward literally anything else—the sudden conviction that you need to check your email, or that this would be a great time to finally organize your desk drawer, or that you should really research the best kind of ergonomic chair before you do anything else—pause for just a second.

That pull? That's not you. That's the machine, doing exactly what it was built to do, trying to route you away from a feeling it has classified as a threat.

And now that you can see it, you get to choose whether to follow it.

Not every time. You won't win every time. The machine is old and well-practiced and faster than conscious thought. But you don't need to win every time. You just need to win often enough that the pattern starts to shift.

Because here's what happens when you start winning those small moments: the machine begins to learn that the thing it classified as a threat isn't actually dangerous. The feeling you've been avoiding is uncomfortable, yes, but it doesn't kill you. And the task on the other side of that feeling—the one you've been putting off—turns out to be just a task, not a referendum on your worth as a human being.

The machine is still there. But it gets a little quieter each time you prove it wrong.

And the next pattern we're going to examine together—the one that probably feels the most familiar, the one you might even take a strange pride in—is the way your brain has learned to make avoidance feel like preparation, and delay feel like strategy.

It's called the Relief Trade, and it's running right now.

The chipped Formica countertop felt cold under Amelia's elbows.

The chipped Formica seemed to absorb Amelia's frustration, a silent witness to the gap between intention and action. The subtle weight of those unmet expectations now hangs over everything she does, an invisible drag on her energy as it shifts towards whatever feels *easiest*.

# Chapter 2 — The Relief Trade

## Why avoiding the task feels like solving something

Studies show the human brain dedicates roughly 43% of waking hours to unintentional thought – daydreaming, worrying, future planning, rehashing the past. This isn't a bug; it's an ancient mechanism designed for pattern recognition and threat assessment, one that often runs amok in the modern world.

But here's the part of that story that doesn't usually get examined: for the entire year leading up to those final seventy-two hours, Urban wasn't sitting still doing nothing. He was busy. He remembers being busy. The year wasn't empty—it was full of other tasks, other projects, a long string of things that genuinely needed doing and genuinely got done. The thesis just wasn't one of them.

That's not a time management problem. If it were, the solution would be simple: block off more hours, protect the time better, schedule it earlier in the day. Those fixes assume the issue is availability—that the task isn't getting done because there isn't room for it. But Urban had a year. The time was there. What wasn't there was the ability to turn toward the task and stay turned toward it long enough to make any real progress, because every time he tried, something in him flinched, and he found himself doing something else instead.

You've done this. I know you have, because I have, and because the seventy million people who've watched that talk have, and because the pattern is so universal it barely needs explaining. You sit down to start the thing that actually matters—the project with your name on it, the conversation you've been putting off, the decision that's been sitting in your inbox for two weeks. You open the file.

You look at it. Maybe four seconds pass.

Then you're somewhere else.

Not dramatically. You didn't storm out of the room or throw your laptop across the floor. You just... drifted. You checked a message that could have waited. You remembered the laundry sitting in the machine. You noticed your desk was cluttered and started tidying it. And here's the strange part: in the moment you turned away, it didn't feel like avoidance. It felt like relief.

That relief is real. That's the part most productivity advice never touches, because if the relief is real—if your nervous system genuinely calms the second your attention leaves the hard task and lands on the easier one—then this isn't a problem you can solve with better planning. It's a problem of what your mind is doing underneath the planning, a trade it's making faster than conscious thought, weighing a small certain relief available right now against a larger uncertain cost that won't land until later.

I caught myself running this exact trade a few years ago, and I only noticed because it went on long enough to become absurd. I had one performance review to write. One. It wasn't a pleasant task—the employee in question had some real issues that needed addressing, and I knew the conversation was going to be uncomfortable—but it also wasn't *hard* in any technical sense. I'd written dozens of reviews before. I knew the format. I had all the information I needed.

I didn't write it.

Instead, I reorganized my entire file system. Not just a quick cleanup—an overhaul. Color-coded folders. Renamed documents. Nested hierarchies for projects I hadn't touched in two years. I did this for three days straight, several hours a day, with the kind of focused intensity I wish I could summon on command for actual important work. And the whole time, some part of me genuinely believed I was being productive. I was solving a problem. The problem just wasn't the one I was supposed to be solving.

On day four, I finally opened the review document, and the moment I did, I felt it—a tightness in my chest, a faint dread, the same feeling that had been quietly steering me toward the file system every time I sat down at my desk. The filing wasn't urgent. It was just *easier*. And easier had been enough to win, three days running, because the part of my brain weighing the options wasn't thinking three days ahead. It was thinking three seconds ahead, and three seconds ahead, color-coding a folder felt better than facing that review.

That's the trade. That's the whole mechanism. And once you see it, you start seeing it everywhere.

---

Most procrastination research for decades treated the problem as a planning failure—poor time management, weak prioritization, an inability to estimate how long tasks actually take. The advice that came out of that framing was predictable: make better schedules, break big projects into smaller pieces, use a timer. All sensible. None of it particularly effective for the kind of procrastination that actually interferes with people's lives, because the kind that interferes isn't about time. It's about feeling.

The psychologist Timothy Pychyl spent years studying procrastination at Carleton University, and what he found, over and over, was that people don't avoid tasks because they don't have time for them. They avoid tasks because thinking about doing the task produces a negative feeling—anxiety, boredom, frustration, overwhelm—and avoiding the task makes that feeling drop. Immediately.

That immediate drop is the reinforcement. It's not a side effect. It's the whole point.

In one of Pychyl's studies, participants carried devices that beeped at random intervals throughout the day, prompting them to report what they were doing and how they were feeling. The pattern was clear: procrastination happened most often when people were in a bad mood and least often when they were in a good one. But here's the kicker—right *after* procrastinating, people's moods improved. Not a lot. Not for long. But reliably. The avoidance worked, at least in the very short term, which is exactly the kind of reinforcement that trains a behavior to keep happening.

Pychyl's collaborator, Fuschia Sirois, pushed this further. She looked at procrastination not as a time management issue but as a form of emotion regulation—a short-term strategy for feeling better *right now*, pursued at the expense of long-term goals. The task itself is rarely the true object of avoidance. The feeling attached to the task is.

Think about Eleanor Roosevelt. She gave hundreds of speeches over her lifetime, became one of the most effective public speakers of her generation, and by all accounts dreaded it every single time. Not the speaking itself, exactly. The *feeling* of inadequacy. The voice in her head insisting she hadn't prepared enough, wasn't articulate enough, would stumble over her words and embarrass herself. Before major addresses, she'd spend hours arranging and rearranging her notes—not because the rearranging improved the speech, but because the act of organizing quieted that voice, at least for a few minutes. She wasn't eliminating the dread. She was just... managing it. Badly, but genuinely.

That's situation modification, in the language of emotion regulation research. The psychologist James Gross, whose work maps out the different strategies people use to manage unwanted feelings, describes situation modification as physically changing your circumstances to avoid a feeling before it fully arrives—closing the laptop, leaving the room, picking up the phone instead of the file. Procrastination, looked at through this lens, is situation modification aimed at a task: you're not managing the project, you're managing your relationship to the feeling the project produces, by removing yourself from its presence as completely and as quickly as you can.

Most of the time, you don't even notice you're doing it. The alternate task you turn to almost always has some genuine merit—laundry that actually needs folding, an email that actually needs a reply, a desk that actually is cluttered. This isn't random. A mind looking for an escape route reliably finds the most respectable-looking one available, because a respectable escape gives you relief *and* an alibi in the same move. You're not avoiding work. You're doing *different* work. Important work, even.

Just not the work that matters.

---

There's an older piece of science underneath all of this, and it explains the timing of the trade with unusual precision. It's called temporal discounting, and it describes the near-universal tendency to weigh something small and immediate far more heavily than something large and delayed.

Most of the research on this was built around money. Offer someone ten dollars today or fifteen dollars in a week, and a surprising number of people take the ten, even though waiting objectively pays better. The delay makes the larger reward feel less real, less compelling. Your brain discounts it.

The psychologist George Ainslie, whose work on impulsiveness helped formalize the math behind this, was explicit that the same curve applies to almost any outcome a mind has to weigh across time—not just money, but pain, pleasure, effort, relief. Applied to procrastination, the curve produces exactly the trade this chapter opened with: a small, certain relief available in the next thirty seconds outweighs a much larger but delayed and abstract cost that won't land until the deadline gets close.

The relief is real and immediate. You can *feel* it in your body—the tightness drops, the pulse slows, the dread lifts. The cost is also real, but it's distant, vague, easy to discount. And a mind wired to discount distant things heavily will choose the relief every single time, unless something interrupts the pattern.

Here's why this is so hard to catch in the moment: the trade doesn't *feel* like giving in. It feels like making a reasonable decision. The laundry genuinely needed doing. The email genuinely needed a reply. You're not being lazy. You're being *practical.* And that story—that you made a sensible choice about priorities—insulates the pattern from scrutiny, because who argues with being practical?

There's a version of this that happens so fast you barely register it. Call it the flinch-and-flee sequence. A task appears in awareness. Your mind runs a split-second appraisal of how engaging with it will *feel.* The appraisal comes back negative. And an alternate action is already underway before the appraisal has even surfaced as a conscious thought.

People who catch themselves mid-sequence describe a strange experience: realizing, several minutes into some other activity, that they don't actually remember *deciding* to do it. They just... ended up there. That's not a failure of attention. It's evidence the whole sequence ran below the level where deliberate choice usually happens, the same way you flinch from a hot stove before you consciously decide to flinch.

A slower, quieter version of the trade plays out over days instead of minutes. Instead of one dramatic escape, you get a long string of small, individually reasonable deferrals. *I'll start after this meeting. I'll start tomorrow when I'm fresher. This week is unusually busy, so next week makes more sense.* Each deferral, examined alone, looks rational. Stacked across three weeks, they produce the exact same outcome as the fast version—the task still isn't done—just with a much better story to explain why it isn't really avoidance at all.

The psychologist Walter Mischel spent decades studying self-regulation, most famously in studies where kids chose between one marshmallow now or two marshmallows if they waited fifteen minutes. The kids who managed to wait weren't just tougher or more disciplined in some vague, general way. They'd found strategies—often without being taught—to keep the tempting object from fully capturing their attention. They looked away. They sang to themselves. They thought about the marshmallow as a cloud instead of a treat.

Mischel's later work described the mind as running two interacting systems: a "hot" system, fast and emotional, that responds to what something feels like *right now*, and a "cool" system, slower and more deliberate, that can think about the same thing more abstractly and weigh it against future considerations. The kids who waited longest weren't out-muscling the hot system once it was already locked onto the marshmallow. They were keeping the cool system engaged *before* the hot system fully activated.

The same principle applies here. You're not going to out-discipline the hot system once it's staring directly at the dreaded task and reaching for the escape hatch. The more reliable move is engaging the cool system *before* the flinch happens—which is exactly what naming the feeling in advance, and deciding the first move ahead of time, are both designed to do.

But here's the part that makes the pattern so durable: every time the trade runs successfully—every time turning away from the hard task makes the bad feeling drop—the pattern gets reinforced. This is basic learning. Rewards that follow an action strengthen the likelihood of that action repeating. And relief is a reward, even if it's bought at the cost of something you care about more.

Which means every single time you run the trade, you're training your own mind, one repetition at a time, that this specific task is something to escape from rather than engage with. The task isn't just sitting there unchanged. It's becoming, gradually, genuinely harder to approach, not because anything about the work itself shifted, but because you've now built an associative link between thinking about it and fleeing from it.

A task you've been avoiding for three months can start to feel almost unapproachable in a way it never did at the beginning, and that's not a metaphor. You've taught yourself, through repetition, to treat it as something threatening.

---

The relief itself isn't the expensive part. A few minutes of relief here and there won't ruin your life. What's expensive is what compounds underneath the relief while you're not looking.

The task doesn't sit quietly while you avoid it. It changes shape.

A difficult conversation that would have been merely uncomfortable in week one has, by week four, accumulated a second layer of discomfort—not just the original issue, but now also the fact that you waited so long. The other person has noticed. They're interpreting the delay, and the interpretation is almost never in your favor. What was once a straightforward "we need to talk about this" is now "we need to talk about this, and also about why you've been avoiding talking about this."

A creative project that would have been merely difficult on day one has, by the time the deadline arrives, shrunk the runway so severely that the version you finally produce is worse than what you were capable of making—not because your ability declined, but because the trade kept eating your time. You don't get to do your best work in the last six hours before something's due. You get to do survival work. Functional, maybe. But not the thing you actually had in you.

I watched this happen to a colleague once, a magazine editor named Sarah. She'd been assigned a dense, difficult biography to review—an artist with a notoriously complicated life, the kind of book that demands real attention. Instead of starting, she began "preparing." She researched the author's other work. She read reviews of similar biographies. She reorganized her desk. She color-coded her notes. Each step felt productive. Important, even. Essential groundwork.

Days became a week. The week became two. The manuscript sat untouched.

When I finally asked her about it, she launched into a detailed explanation of all the prep work she'd done, and it sounded impressive. Diligent. Almost heroic. But underneath, barely visible, was quiet panic. The biography felt overwhelming, and she'd built an elaborate system of delay to avoid confronting that feeling. Each careful step wasn't preparation. It was relief, dressed up as responsibility.

There's a version of the cost that's harder to see because it doesn't show up in missed deadlines or unfinished projects. It shows up in how you feel about yourself.

Every time you run the trade—every time you sit down intending to do the thing and then don't—you're not just delaying the task. You're logging evidence, internally, about what kind of person you are. Evidence that you don't follow through. Evidence that you can't be trusted, even by yourself, to do what you said you'd do.

That evidence accumulates. Slowly. Quietly. And after enough repetitions, it starts shaping how you see yourself in ways that go far beyond the original task. You stop thinking of yourself as someone who's currently struggling with one particular project and start thinking of yourself as someone who just... doesn't finish things. That shift, from a specific behavioral pattern to a fixed identity, is one of the most corrosive long-term costs the relief trade produces, because once it's an identity, it starts feeling true in a way that's much harder to argue with.

And here's the truly expensive part: that self-concept begins shaping what you attempt in the first place. If you're someone who doesn't finish things, why start the novel? Why apply for the job? Why have the conversation? The avoidance spreads backward in time, from tasks you've started to tasks you never let yourself begin, because the trade has now taught you that engaging with hard things leads to failure, and it's less painful to just not engage at all.

There's a physiological cost too, one that explains why the relief the trade delivers feels so immediate and so hard to argue with. The negative feeling attached to an aversive task shows up as a real, bodily state—tightness in your chest, faster pulse, shallow breathing, a subtle bracing. And the alternate activity you turn to interrupts that state within *seconds*. Not minutes. Seconds.

This isn't metaphorical. Your nervous system genuinely calms. And a body that's just been given relief has very little patience for an argument about long-term consequences it can't feel yet.

There's also a version of the cost that lands on the people around you, not just on you. A partner watching you repeatedly choose the easier task over the one that matters can't see the flinch, the appraisal, the split-second escape. They only see the outcome: the thing not happening, again. Left unexplained, this reads as carelessness, or a lack of follow-through, and it quietly erodes trust in ways that are hard to repair later.

Naming the mechanism to the people closest to you isn't about making excuses. It's about offering a map to what's happening underneath the behavior, so they're not left filling in the blanks with the worst interpretation. It won't erase their frustration. But it does shift the story from "they don't care" to "they're stuck," and stuck is something people can work with in a way carelessness isn't.

There's one more cost, and it's the one that does the most damage over the truly long run: the task you avoid for long enough starts to feel *timeless*. Like it's always been there. A permanent fixture of your mental background instead of something with an actual, traceable starting date.

This distortion matters because it makes the task feel less solvable than it is. A problem that feels eternal and vague is much harder to imagine tackling than a problem you can date to six weeks ago—a specific, bounded stretch of avoidance rather than an unchangeable condition of your life. Part of what makes naming the pattern useful, beyond interrupting the trade in the moment, is restoring an accurate sense of scale. This isn't forever. It's six weeks. And six weeks is a length of time a deliberate override can very plausibly outlast.

---

So what do you actually *do* about it?

Not in some distant, aspirational future where you've somehow become a different person with perfect discipline. Monday. What do you do Monday?

First: name the feeling *before* the task appears. Not during the flinch—by then the hot system's already engaged and the escape route is already opening. *Before*. Sit down for thirty seconds the night before, or the morning of, and finish this sentence out loud: "When I think about starting [the task], the feeling that comes up is __________."

Boredom. Dread. Overwhelm. Inadequacy. Frustration. Whatever it is, name it specifically. Say it out loud if you can, because saying something out loud pulls it out of the vague emotional fog and into the realm of things you can examine. You're not trying to make the feeling go away—you can't, and trying to will just add a layer of frustration on top of the original feeling. You're trying to *see* it clearly, so that when it shows up in the moment, you recognize it for what it is: a feeling, not a fact about the task.

Second: decide the first move in advance. Not the whole project. Not even the first hour. The first *move*. The single, specific, physical action you will take to begin. Open the file. Write one sentence. Read the first page of the brief. Make the call. One move, concrete enough that you'll know within five seconds whether you've done it.

Write it down. "Tomorrow at 9, I will open the document and write one sentence." The specificity matters. Vague intentions—"I'll make progress on the project"—give the avoidant system too much room to negotiate. A concrete move is harder to argue with.

Third: when the feeling arrives—and it will—don't fight it. You're not trying to be brave or tough or powered by willpower. You're trying to do the move you decided on *while the feeling is still there*. The feeling doesn't have to go away first. You don't have to feel ready. You just have to do the move.

This will feel deeply uncomfortable. That's fine. Uncomfortable is not the same as unbearable, and the difference matters. Let the discomfort be there. Notice it. Notice that you're doing the thing anyway.

What you're doing, in that moment, is running a different kind of trade. You're teaching your mind, through direct experience, that engaging with the task while the bad feeling is present doesn't lead to catastrophe. It just leads to... the next sentence. The next paragraph. The thing moving forward, slightly, while you feel bad. That's the new evidence you're building. Not that you're suddenly good at this. Not that it feels great. Just that it's *doable*, even when it doesn't feel good.

Fourth: make the task more concrete, especially if it's been sitting vague and enormous in your mind for weeks. Vague tasks are inherently more aversive because your mind doesn't know what "work on the project" actually entails, so it imagines the hardest, most overwhelming version and recoils from *that*.

Break it down. Not into a beautiful, perfectly sequenced project plan—that's just productive procrastination wearing a disguise. Into the next two or three things that have to happen for the project to move. Write those down. Pick one. Do that one.

"Clean the garage" never happens. "Put the three boxes by the door in the car" does. The difference isn't effort. It's specificity.

Fifth—and this one's harder to hear, but it's important—stop waiting for the task to feel manageable before you start. It won't. That's the whole problem. The feeling is the thing you're avoiding, and the feeling doesn't go away just because you stared at your to-do list harder or made a better plan. The only way through is to start *while it still feels bad*, and discover, through doing it, that you can tolerate the bad feeling long enough to make progress anyway.

You might be thinking this sounds exhausting. It is, at first. But here's what's more exhausting: running the same internal negotiation every single morning about whether today's the day, losing that negotiation every single time, and carrying the task—unchanged, growing heavier—into tomorrow. That's the hidden cost the relief trade never shows you up front. The relief lasts thirty seconds. The weight lasts all day.

The pattern isn't permanent. It's learned. And anything learned can be interrupted, then gradually unlearned, one deliberate override at a time. You're not trying to become someone who never feels dread or boredom or overwhelm when a hard task appears. You're trying to become someone who feels it and starts anyway, because you've built enough evidence, through small, repeated moves, that starting doesn't require the feeling to go away first.

Monday, pick one task you've been avoiding. Name the feeling. Decide the first move. Do the move while the feeling is still there.

That's it. That's the whole mechanism running in reverse.

And if it works even once—if you get one sentence down, one call made, one file opened—you've just run a trade in the other direction. A small, uncomfortable action now, in exchange for a much larger sense of capability later. That's the trade worth making. Not because it feels good in the moment.

Because of what it builds.

What you're building isn't confidence in the traditional sense—the kind that arrives like a weather front and makes everything feel possible. You're building something closer to evidence. A small, private ledger of moments when you felt the resistance and moved anyway. When the discomfort was present and you didn't wait for it to dissolve before starting.

This matters because the traditional story about confidence puts it in the wrong order. It suggests you need to *feel* capable before you *act* capable. That you should wait until the dread lifts, until you're in the right headspace, until you've psyched yourself up enough. But that sequence keeps you stuck, because the feeling rarely arrives on cue. And even when it does, it's unreliable. It comes and goes based on sleep, blood sugar, whether someone cut you off in traffic.

The ledger you're building works differently. It doesn't care how you felt. It only tracks what you did. And over time, that ledger becomes the thing you consult when the next hard task appears. Not "Do I feel ready?" but "Have I done this before—started while it felt bad?" And if the answer is yes, even once, you have a data point. If it's yes ten times, you have a pattern. At some point, the pattern becomes more convincing than the feeling.

This is why the first reversal is so important. Not because one sentence written or one email sent changes your life. But because it creates the first entry. And once there's one, there can be two. Once there are two, there can be ten. The mechanism you've been running—trading action for temporary relief—has been writing its own ledger this whole time. A long list of moments when you chose the feeling over the move. That ledger has weight. It's shaped how you see yourself. What you're doing now is starting a second ledger. A competing one. And at first, it's going to be much shorter. But length isn't the only variable. Recency matters. Direction matters. The trajectory of the last ten entries matters more than the sum of the last thousand.

If the last ten times you faced a hard task, you avoided it, that's your working theory of who you are. If the last ten times you faced a hard task, you started it anyway—even badly, even while feeling dread—that's a different theory. And theories shape behavior. Not because they're true in some absolute sense, but because they're the story you're currently telling about what happens when you encounter resistance.

The other thing that builds, quietly, is your tolerance for the feeling itself. Not that it gets smaller. Not that you learn to enjoy it. But that it stops functioning as a stop sign. Most of us treat emotional discomfort as diagnostic. If it feels bad, something must be wrong. If it feels this bad, I must not be ready. If I were supposed to do this, it wouldn't feel like this. But that's not how discomfort works. Discomfort is just the activation cost of doing something unfamiliar, or something with stakes, or something you've been putting off long enough that it's accumulated weight. It's not a message. It's not a warning. It's just the texture of the moment before you start.

Once you've started while feeling it enough times, the feeling loses its veto power. It's still there. It still feels bad. But it no longer gets to decide whether you move. That's a different kind of freedom than "feeling good about it." It's the freedom to act even when the feeling says don't. And that might be the only kind of freedom that actually compounds. Because the things worth doing—worth building, worth saying, worth trying—don't wait for you to feel ready. They just wait for you to start.

So what happens after Monday? After you've picked one task, named the feeling, and done the first move?

You do it again Tuesday. Not because Monday felt good. Maybe it didn't. Maybe it felt exactly as bad as you thought it would, and the thing you produced was mediocre, and the discomfort didn't even fade afterward. That's fine. You're not trying to make it feel good. You're trying to make it repeatable. And repeatable doesn't mean easy. It just means doable. You can do hard things more than once. That's the only requirement.

What you'll notice, if you keep going, is that the delay shrinks. Not every time. Not in a straight line. But over weeks, the time between "I should do this" and "I'm doing this" gets shorter. The negotiation phase—the part where you debate whether now is the right time, whether you're in the right mood, whether you should wait until after lunch—compresses. Not because you've stopped having the debate, but because you've stopped letting it run the clock. You know where it goes. You've heard all the arguments. They don't get more convincing with repetition. So you start while they're still talking.

And eventually, something shifts that's hard to describe but easy to feel. The task is still hard. The feeling is still uncomfortable. But you're no longer *in relationship* with the discomfort the same way. You're not trying to negotiate with it, or outsmart it, or wait for it to leave. You're just acknowledging it's there, the way you'd acknowledge weather, and moving anyway. It's there because you're doing something that matters. That's the deal. And you've decided the deal is worth it.

That's what the relief trade was costing you. Not just the work you didn't do. But the evidence you didn't gather. The ledger you didn't build. The small, steady proof that you're someone who can feel the feeling and start anyway.

You still are. You always were. You just have to trade in the other direction long enough to remember.

…trading long-term progress for momentary peace.

Tim Urban's story isn't just funny; it reveals something fundamental about how we bargain with ourselves, trading long-term progress for momentary peace.

The procrastinator's schedule looks productive to everyone else. You rearrange. You optimize. You research better methods for doing the thing you're not doing. You build scaffolding around a structure that doesn't exist yet. And each of those acts delivers a small dose of resolution—the feeling that you've handled it, that you're no longer the person ignoring the problem.

Except you are. You're just ignoring it more elaborately.

The relief trade doesn't announce itself. It doesn't show up wearing a sign that says "distraction" or "avoidance." It arrives dressed as progress. As reasonable prioritization. As taking care of something else that also matters. And because it delivers real relief—because the discomfort genuinely decreases when you switch tasks—it's easy to mistake the trade for a solution.

That's the trap. Relief feels like resolution. The absence of discomfort feels like the presence of progress. Your nervous system can't tell the difference between "I'm no longer anxious because I handled it" and "I'm no longer anxious because I stopped looking at it." Both register as problem solved.

So you keep trading. And the pattern deepens.

What makes it particularly insidious is that the relief trade borrows credibility from real self-care. Sometimes you genuinely do need to step back. Sometimes the right move is to put something down, let your nervous system reset, and return with fresh perspective. Rest isn't avoidance. Strategic delay isn't procrastination. There are moments when the most productive thing you can do is stop.

But the relief trade mimics that wisdom. It wears the language of self-compassion while serving a completely different function. It's not rest. It's not strategic. It's the immediate discharge of discomfort at the expense of the thing that would actually resolve it.

And because it borrows the vocabulary of healthy boundaries—"I'm listening to my body," "I'm not forcing it," "I'm honoring my energy"—it's almost impossible to argue with. Who's going to tell you that listening to yourself is wrong?

No one. Because it's not wrong. It's just not what you're doing.

What you're doing is offering your discomfort a bribe. You're saying: I'll give you relief right now if you stop making noise. And your discomfort takes the deal every time, because that's how discomfort works. It doesn't have a long-term strategy. It just wants out.

The problem is that the thing generating the discomfort is still there. The unwritten email. The unscheduled appointment. The conversation you're avoiding. The project you haven't started. Whatever it is, it's still sitting in the background, accruing weight. And because you've trained yourself to interpret relief as resolution, you don't realize that the trade just made the problem bigger.

Not immediately. That's what makes it sustainable.

If the consequences showed up right away, you'd stop. If avoiding the thing hurt more than doing the thing, the pattern wouldn't persist. But relief trades are built on delay. The cost is always later. The benefit is always now. And human beings are breathtakingly bad at weighing delayed costs against immediate comfort.

So the cycle continues. The task sits. The discomfort builds. You trade it away. The relief arrives. The task remains. The discomfort returns, slightly heavier. You trade again.

And somewhere in that loop, you stop noticing that the thing you're avoiding isn't actually getting harder—it's your tolerance for discomfort that's getting lower. The task is the same size it always was. You've just made yourself more sensitive to the feeling of not having done it.

That's what breaks people. Not the size of the thing. The inability to sit with the feeling of the thing undone.

And the relief trade makes it worse, because every time you opt out, you reinforce the idea that the discomfort is intolerable. You teach yourself that this particular flavor of unease is something you can't handle. That you need an exit. That the only reasonable response is to step away.

Which means the next time it shows up, it arrives with proof. Last time, you couldn't do it. Last time, you needed relief. Last time, the feeling was too much.

And it becomes true, not because the task got harder, but because you've been training yourself to believe the feeling is unbearable.

That's the hidden cost. The relief trade doesn't just delay the work. It erodes your confidence that you're capable of doing hard things. Every trade is a small vote of no confidence in your own ability to tolerate discomfort. Every avoided task is evidence that you're not the kind of person who can push through.

And evidence compounds.

You don't just lose time. You lose trust in yourself. You lose the internal knowledge that you can do difficult things, that you can feel uncomfortable and move anyway, that you're someone who keeps promises to yourself even when it's hard.

That's what makes the relief trade so expensive. It's not the missed deadline. It's the slow dissolution of the belief that you're the kind of person who meets them.

And once that belief is gone, everything gets harder. Because now you're not just doing the task. You're doing it against the accumulated evidence that you can't. You're fighting your own history. And that's a battle the relief trade has been quietly setting up for months.

The way out isn't discipline. It's not forcing yourself to suffer. It's not punishing yourself for taking relief or shaming yourself for avoiding discomfort.

The way out is smaller. And stranger.

It's noticing, in real time, when the relief is a trade and not a solution. It's catching the moment when you're about to pivot away from the thing and asking: is this rest, or is this relief?

Rest restores. Relief just pauses.

He remembers being busy. The year wasn't empty—it was full of other tasks, other projects, a long string of things that kept the 'instant gratification monkey' occupied.

Tim Urban's TED Talk resonated because it visually captured the feeling, but didn't delve into *why* that internal 'instant gratification monkey' is so powerful. The surprising truth about those hours spent not fully present may be less about wandering minds and more about a deeply ingrained survival mechanism.

# Chapter 3 — The Perfect Start

## Why the project that matters most is the one you can't seem to begin

Do you ever find yourself meticulously *preparing* to do something—organizing your desk, researching tools, making endless lists—but never actually starting? It's a common experience, but rarely understood as what it is: a carefully constructed defense against feeling uncomfortable.

She'd bought the fruit intending to 'get healthy,' another promise made with hopeful energy—a basket now sitting on the counter, slowly browning, mirroring the faded ambition behind this speaking pitch.

I did not write the pitch that first week. Or the second.

Instead, I reorganized my entire portfolio. Every project description got rewritten—twice, sometimes three times. I studied recordings of past speakers, took notes on their cadence, their slide design, the way they opened with a story and landed on a principle. I made a spreadsheet. I'm not exaggerating. I literally made a spreadsheet tracking the common visual themes across the past eighteen months of decks I could find online, cross-referencing fonts and color palettes like I was preparing a graduate thesis on conference aesthetics rather than writing a three-minute pitch about my own work.

Each evening I'd close my laptop and tell myself this was *preparation.* That a brilliant pitch couldn't be built on shaky foundations. That the work I was doing now—studying, organizing, analyzing—was the necessary groundwork for the real thing, which

I'd get to soon. Tomorrow, probably. Definitely by this weekend.

By week three, the deadline bearing down like weather I could feel in my chest, I felt *less* prepared than when I'd started. The other speakers—past and future—seemed to operate on a different plane. They had this ease, this fluency, this way of standing in front of a room that suggested they'd earned their place there. My own work, laid out in that meticulously organized portfolio, looked thinner somehow. Less significant. Not quite ready for that kind of scrutiny.

So I didn't submit anything.

A perfectly good opportunity evaporated. Someone else got the slot—a designer whose work I admired but whose portfolio, I knew for a fact, was less polished than mine. She just sent the pitch. She didn't spend two weeks studying slide deck fonts. She didn't make a spreadsheet. She wrote three paragraphs about her work and hit send, and they said yes.

It's easy to tell yourself stories about why you don't start. You need more information, better tools, a clearer vision, a stronger hook. These reasons feel responsible, diligent. But what if the problem isn't a failure of planning? What if you're not stuck because you don't know *how* to begin, but because some part of you has decided that beginning—actually putting something imperfect into the world—is the real threat?

---

Sarah designed album covers for indie labels. Good ones. The kind that ended up in design blogs, that musicians specifically requested her for. When a label sent her a brief—deadline, dimensions, mood board, budget—she'd turn around a concept in three days that usually got approved on first review. She wasn't slow.

She wasn't indecisive. She could look at someone else's creative vision and make it sing.

But her own website had been "in progress" for two and a half years when I met her.

Not because she didn't have the skills. She could code, she could design, she had more than enough finished work to showcase. The problem was that her website wasn't someone else's vision—it was hers. It had to represent *her*, which meant it had to be perfect, or at least perfect enough to withstand the kind of judgment she imagined design peers would bring to it. Every time she sat down to build it, she'd start with the typography. Spend an hour testing font pairings. Land on something that felt right, then open it the next day and decide it felt generic, or too trendy, or not trendy enough. Start over. Move to color. Build a palette. Scrap it. The site never launched because the site could never be good enough to deserve launching, and as long as it stayed unbuilt, it remained a perfect idea rather than a flawed reality.

She wasn't procrastinating in the traditional sense—she was *working*. Just not on the part that mattered. Mood boards, yes. Font tests, absolutely. Sketches and wireframes and inspiration folders organized by aesthetic movement. The actual building of the thing? That required shipping something imperfect, and imperfect meant visible, and visible meant exposed to the exact judgment she'd been avoiding by staying in the planning phase.

This pattern isn't rare. It's everywhere. The entrepreneur who's been refining the pitch deck for eighteen months but hasn't talked to a single potential customer. The home cook who owns four sous vide machines and a $900 knife set but won't host a dinner party because the execution might not match the vision. The parent who's been "working on" a children's book for three years, by which they mean thinking about it a lot and occasionally writing an opening paragraph before deleting it and starting over with a different tone.

The common thread isn't that these people lack skill or ambition. It's that the project *matters*. There are real stakes. These aren't tasks you can knock out on autopilot, fire off without a second thought, delegate to a quiet Tuesday afternoon between meetings. They require something more vulnerable: putting a piece of yourself into the world and allowing other people to form opinions about it. And that exposure—that moment when the thing stops being a private thought experiment and becomes a public object—triggers a freeze that has almost nothing to do with time management and everything to do with what happens inside your nervous system when it perceives a threat.

Because here's what most productivity advice gets wrong: procrastination isn't a planning problem. It's an emotional regulation problem wearing a planning problem's clothes. You don't delay the work because you can't *organize* your time. You delay it because you can't *tolerate* the feeling that starting produces—the discomfort of not knowing if it'll be good, the anxiety of imagining judgment, the fear that the gap between your vision and your ability is wider than you can admit. These aren't rational obstacles you can schedule your way around. They're warning signals from a part of your brain that genuinely believes starting the project is dangerous.

Not dangerous like crossing a busy street. Dangerous like exposing yourself to a judgment that could confirm your deepest fear: that you're not as capable as you'd hoped.

---

The psychologists Gordon Flett and Paul Hewitt have spent decades studying perfectionism, and one of their core findings—one that surprises people who think of perfectionism as just "having high standards"—is that perfectionism and procrastination aren't opposites. They're traveling companions. Often they're the same behavior, looked at from two different angles.

Flett and Hewitt distinguish between self-oriented perfectionism, which is about the standards you set for yourself, and socially prescribed perfectionism, which is about the standards you believe others hold for you. Both correlate strongly with procrastination, but not for the reason you'd expect. It's not that perfectionists are lazy or avoidant by nature. It's that when you've internalized the belief that anything less than perfect is fundamentally threatening—to your self-worth, to your reputation, to your identity as someone competent—you'll do almost anything to delay the moment when imperfection becomes visible.

An unstarted project can remain perfect indefinitely. It lives in the realm of potential, where it can have every quality you've ever hoped for. It only becomes flawed—provably, undeniably flawed—the moment you begin. The moment words go on the page, the moment the design takes shape, the moment the code compiles and runs and reveals itself to be slower or buggier or less elegant than you'd imagined. Starting transforms the perfect imagined thing into an imperfect real thing, and for someone who has learned to equate imperfection with danger, that transformation is worth avoiding at enormous cost.

This is why the freeze hits hardest on the projects that matter most. Not because they're harder in any technical sense—often they're well within your skill range—but because the stakes are higher. A client project has a clear brief and a deadline and someone else's vision guiding it. Your own project? That's yours. If it fails, if it's mediocre, if it lands with a thud, there's no one else to blame. The judgment falls on you. And if you've structured your self-worth around being someone who produces good work, that judgment feels like it's evaluating *you*, not just the thing you made.

So you prepare instead. You research. You organize. You refine the outline, test the tools, study the masters, build the foundation. All of that feels productive—and some of it *is* productive, up to a point—but there's a moment when preparation stops serving the work and starts serving the avoidance. When reading one more article or adjusting the outline one more time yields almost no new insight but successfully delays the moment when you have to create something real and imperfect and subject to judgment.

The tell is usually the ratio. If you've spent four weeks preparing for a task that would take two days to complete, and each new round of preparation produces less useful information than the last, preparation has quietly become the thing you're doing *instead* of the work, not the thing you're doing *before* it.

---

You might be thinking this doesn't quite describe you. Maybe you don't see yourself as a perfectionist—you're fine with mistakes, you believe in iteration, you tell people all the time that done is better than perfect. And maybe that's true. Maybe you genuinely don't fear failure in the traditional sense.

But perfectionism doesn't always show up as fear of failure. Sometimes it presents as an inability to tolerate *mediocrity*. A refusal to release anything into the world that isn't exceptional. You're not afraid your work will be *bad*—you're afraid it'll be *fine*. Competent but unremarkable. Good enough to avoid embarrassment but not good enough to matter. And if you've built your identity around doing work that stands out, around being someone whose contributions are valuable and distinct, "fine" feels worse than nothing.

This version is harder to spot because it sounds like high standards, which we're taught to value. It sounds like caring about quality, like refusing to settle, like respecting your audience enough not to waste their time with half-baked ideas. But the effect is identical to the more obvious version: the bar gets set so high that almost nothing can clear it on a first attempt, and because first attempts are the only way forward, you stay frozen.

Carol Dweck's research on mindset helps explain why some people recover from a rough first draft easily while others treat it as devastating evidence. Dweck distinguishes between a fixed mindset—the belief that your abilities are essentially stable and unchanging—and a growth mindset—the belief that ability develops through effort and practice. In a fixed-mindset frame, a rough first draft isn't just a rough first draft. It's information about who you are. About a limitation that might be permanent. If the first version comes out clunky or unclear or less brilliant than you'd hoped, that's not just a stage in the process—it's a signal that maybe you're not as good at this as you thought.

Under a growth mindset, that same rough draft means almost nothing. Of course it's rough. First drafts are rough. That's what they're for. The roughness isn't a verdict on your ability; it's a natural part of getting from zero to something real. The draft improves through revision, through feedback, through iterating against reality. The initial version is just the material you need in order to have something to improve.

The perfectionism freeze and the fixed mindset tend to travel together, each one reinforcing the other. High standards make the first draft feel more consequential. A fixed interpretation of any imperfection confirms your fears. This creates a loop: the work feels high-stakes, so you delay starting; delaying means you never get the feedback that would help you improve; lack of improvement seems to confirm that you're not cut out for this; and the whole cycle tightens.

The cost of this pattern goes far beyond missed deadlines. It erodes confidence, because every delay becomes more evidence that you're not the kind of person who follows through. It prevents skill development, because skill grows through iterating against real feedback, and you can't get feedback on work that doesn't exist yet. It strains relationships, because people who depend on you start to learn that your promises come with an asterisk. And it creates a strange, quiet ache—the feeling of carrying around unrealized potential that never gets the chance to become something real.

The unstarted masterpiece remains a masterpiece only in the sense that it never risks becoming anything less. You trade the discomfort of creating something imperfect for the safety of keeping the fantasy intact. But that trade has a price, and the price is that you never find out what you're actually capable of.

---

There's a version of you that handles small tasks without any internal drama. The quick email. The minor calendar update. The errand you knock out in ten minutes on your way home. None of that gets avoided. None of it requires an elaborate plan or a pep talk or three hours of mental preparation. You just do it.

Then there's the other version: the one that opens the document for the project that actually matters, reads the first line from last time, decides it isn't quite right, deletes it, stares at the blank space where it used to be, and closes the laptop. You tell yourself you'll come back to it once you have a clearer sense of direction. Once the vision sharpens. Once you feel more ready.

That clearer sense never arrives through waiting. The vision doesn't sharpen on its own. And "ready" isn't a feeling that descends from the sky—it's something you build by starting before you feel ready, producing something imperfect, and discovering that the imperfection didn't kill you.

The difference between the task you breeze through and the one you avoid has almost nothing to do with difficulty. Often the avoided task is well within your ability. The difference is stakes. The quick email doesn't mean anything about who you are. The project with your name on it? That one could be judged. That one could fail in a way that reflects on you. That one requires tolerating the gap between the perfect version in your head and the messy reality of what you can produce right now, today, with the skills and time and clarity you currently have rather than the ones you wish you had.

And here's the trap: you've quietly made "good enough to start" and "good enough to be judged" the same threshold. But they're not the same. Not even close. Good enough to start means it doesn't have to be brilliant yet—it just has to exist so you have something to work with. Good enough to be judged is the bar for the finished thing, after revision, after feedback, after you've had a chance to close the gap between vision and execution. Conflating those two standards is like refusing to take a single step until you can already see the destination. It guarantees you'll stay exactly where you are.

A small example, but one that stuck with me: I know a writer who spent six months "getting ready" to draft a book proposal. She read other proposals, studied the format, talked to agents, outlined and re-outlined. When she finally sat down to write, she produced the first draft in a weekend. The six months weren't about needing more information. They were about delaying the moment when she'd have to produce something that could be evaluated and found wanting. The information-gathering looked like diligence, but it functioned as protection.

Preparation has a point of diminishing returns, and that point arrives much sooner than it feels like it should. At some stage, further research stops adding clarity and starts adding delay. Another article won't answer the question you're actually stuck on, which isn't "what should I do" but "what if I do it and it isn't good enough." That question doesn't get resolved through more preparation. It gets resolved by doing the thing, surviving the discomfort of it being imperfect, and learning that imperfection is survivable.

---

There's a subtler version of this that shows up late in the process, and it catches people off guard because they think they've already escaped the trap. You've done the work. The project is ninety percent finished. Maybe ninety-five percent. You can see the end from where you're sitting. And then…you stop.

Not because you're stuck. Not because you don't know what the last five percent needs. You know exactly what it needs. You just can't seem to make yourself do it.

This is the same mechanism, just relocated. The almost-finished project now carries all the weight of expectation. It's no longer about avoiding a bad start—it's about avoiding a disappointing finish. As long as it stays ninety percent done, it remains full of potential. You can still tell yourself it'll be great once you polish it, once you add that final section, once you send it out into the world. But the moment you finish it, the moment you hit send or publish or present, it becomes fixed. Judgeable. Subject to the reality of whether it's actually as good as you'd hoped.

So you delay. You find small tasks that need doing first. You tweak things that were already fine. You discover new angles that "really should be included" before you can call it done, even though you know—you *know*—that you're stalling.

The relief isn't in starting. It's in staying safely unfinished.

---

Let me tell you what happens on the other side of the freeze, when you actually start despite the discomfort.

You write the first paragraph and it's not great. Of course it isn't. First paragraphs are almost never great. You keep going anyway. The second paragraph is a little better. The third one finds a rhythm. By the end of the session you've produced something—maybe five hundred words, maybe a page, maybe a rough sketch of the whole thing—and it's imperfect in exactly the ways you feared it would be. Clunky in places. Unclear in others. Definitely not ready to show anyone.

And the world does not end.

That gap between your vision and your execution? It's still there. But now you have something real to work with. You can revise a bad first draft. You can't revise a blank page. The perfectionism told you that starting would expose your inadequacy, and it was half right—starting *did* produce something imperfect. But the part it got wrong, the part that matters, is that the imperfection wasn't a verdict. It was just a stage. The natural, expected, entirely normal stage of making something that doesn't exist yet.

You send the draft to a friend, or a colleague, or just read it yourself the next morning with fresh eyes. You see what works and what doesn't. You fix the things that are fixable, accept the things that are good enough, and move forward. The project that felt impossibly large when it was still imaginary becomes manageable once it's real, because real things can be evaluated and improved and finished, while imaginary perfect things just stay imaginary.

The skill you actually need—the one that matters more than talent or intelligence or taste—is the ability to tolerate creating something bad on the way to creating something good. To sit with the discomfort of the gap. To start before you're ready, produce before you're confident, share before it's perfect. Not because perfection doesn't matter, but because perfection only becomes possible *after* you've created something imperfect to refine.

Every person whose work you admire went through this. The album you love started as a rough demo that sounded nothing like the final version. The book that changed your thinking went through drafts the author would be embarrassed to show you. The product you use every day launched in a form that was missing half the features it has now. None of those things got better by staying unstarted. They got better by being started badly and improved through iteration.

What you're calling "not ready" is often just the feeling of being at the beginning, where everyone starts, where the gap is widest and most uncomfortable. That feeling doesn't go away through waiting. It goes away through starting, and discovering that starting badly is not the same as failing.

---

So what do you actually *do* with this? If the freeze is an emotional regulation problem disguised as a planning problem, what's the

Monday-morning move that gets you unstuck?

First: notice the pattern. Not in a vague "I should probably start that thing" way, but specifically. Which project have you been avoiding? Not delaying because you're busy—avoiding despite having time. The one where you've done everything *around* the work without doing the work itself. Name it. Write it down if that helps make it real.

Second: find the smallest possible version of starting. Not the full project. Not even the first real milestone. The smallest unit of forward motion that counts as beginning. If it's a book, that might be one paragraph. If it's a business, it might be a single conversation with a potential customer. If it's a personal project, it might be opening the file and adding one sentence, even if that sentence is bad. The goal isn't to produce something good. The goal is to produce something *real*, because real is the only thing you can iterate on.

Third—and this is the part that matters—start it badly. On purpose. Give yourself permission to make it worse than you're capable of, just to get it out of your head and onto the page. Set a timer for ten minutes and write without editing. Sketch without worrying about composition. Code without optimizing. The point is to create the conditions where imperfection is expected, even encouraged, so the part of your brain that's been screaming warnings about judgment has nothing left to protect you from. You've already admitted it's going to be bad. Now it can't hurt you.

What you'll probably find—what almost everyone finds—is that once you're past the first few minutes, the work stops feeling quite so threatening. The perfectionism loses its grip, not because your standards changed, but because you're no longer in the high-stakes moment of deciding whether to start. You've already started. Now it's just work. Imperfect, improvable, normal work.

Fourth: take the thing you've made—the bad paragraph, the rough sketch, the ten-minute brain dump—and do something with it before the voice that wants to delete it gets too loud. Send it to someone you trust. Save it with a date stamp so you have a record. Schedule the next session where you'll build on it. Create a commitment that makes it harder to retreat back into the safety of not-yet-started.

The freeze doesn't disappear all at once. You'll still feel the pull to delay, to prepare more, to wait for better conditions. But each time you start despite the discomfort, the pattern weakens. You build evidence that starting badly is survivable. That the gap between vision and execution is normal, not disqualifying. That the judgment you feared either doesn't come, or comes and turns out to be less devastating than staying stuck.

The project that's been sitting untouched for months? It doesn't need a better plan. It needs you to open the file and add one imperfect sentence. Tomorrow you can add another. By the end of the week you'll have something rough and real, which is infinitely more useful than a perfect idea that never left your head.

---

Here's what I didn't tell you about that speaking opportunity: six months later, they opened a second application cycle. This time I wrote the pitch in one sitting. It wasn't brilliant. The opening was weak, the structure was a little wobbly, and I sent it knowing it was flawed. They accepted it anyway. Turns out the thing I'd been afraid of—submitting something imperfect—was never the actual barrier. The barrier was the story I'd told myself about what imperfect meant.

The talk I ended up giving was better than the pitch. Not because I'd waited until I was ready, but because I'd started before I was, and used the feedback from reality to close the gap. The pitch got me in the room. The preparation I did *after* that—once I had a real deadline and real stakes—was focused and useful in a way that two weeks of pre-pitch portfolio reorganization never was.

The difference wasn't talent or skill or even confidence. It was the willingness to let the thing be imperfect long enough to make it better.

You already know what project you've been avoiding. You know what it would look like to start it badly. The question isn't whether you're capable—you are. The question is whether you're willing to tolerate the discomfort of being a beginner at something that matters, of producing work that doesn't match your vision yet, of being seen before you're ready.

That discomfort is the price of making anything real. You can keep paying the cost of avoidance—the quiet ache of unrealized potential, the missed opportunities, the sense that you're capable of more than you're producing—or you can pay the cost of starting: the temporary discomfort of imperfection on the way to something that actually exists.

One of those costs compounds. The other one pays off.

You don't need better conditions. You need to open the file and write the bad first sentence. Do that, and everything else becomes possible. Avoid it, and nothing changes.

The file is still there. It's been there the whole time. What happens next isn't about whether you're ready. It's about whether you're willing to start anyway.

She knew the conference wasn't *about* speaking; it was about proving something to herself, a need that felt both urgent and impossibly distant.

Every project description got rewritten—twice, sometimes three times.

The meticulously rewritten portfolio projects felt…safe. That safety, however, came at the cost of actual momentum, leaving her trapped in a cycle of preparation that never quite reached execution – as if building an elaborate fortress around the thing she actually wanted to achieve.

# Chapter 4 — The Pressure Myth

## Why "I work better under a deadline" almost never holds up to a real look

The chipped Formica countertop felt cold under Leo Maxwell's forearm. 3:17 AM. The kitchen lights hummed, too bright. Around him: glue sticks, tiny plastic cannons, a half-assembled diorama of the Battle of Gettysburg that was supposed to be for his son Ethan's fifth grade history project but had somehow become an indictment of every last-minute choice Leo had made in the past decade.

Two weeks ago, when Ethan brought home the assignment sheet, it had sounded charming. Father-son bonding. A chance to teach through making. Leo even bought extra supplies—the good kind, from the art store.

Now, staring at a lopsided Union line made of popsicle sticks and cotton balls meant to represent cannon smoke, Leo wasn't sure what he was teaching his son. Probably that important projects get done in frantic midnight sessions fueled by panic and cold pizza.

The thing is, he *would* pull it off. He always did. The diorama would get finished, Ethan would turn it in, maybe even get a decent grade. Leo was good at this particular magic trick—conjuring acceptable results from impossibly compressed timeframes. "I thrive under deadlines," he'd say at work, usually while explaining why he hadn't started the quarterly report until the night before it was due.

But sitting there, hot-gluing a miniature Confederate flag to a toothpick at three in the morning, a thought crept in that he'd been avoiding for months: what if the reason he kept doing this had nothing to do with thriving?

I've been that person. My version involved a conference presentation I rewrote entirely on a red-eye flight to Boston, working with such manic focus that the woman next to me asked if I was okay. And I told myself the same story Leo told himself: that the pressure sharpened me, that my best work emerged when the clock was ticking.

Except when I gave that presentation—which went fine, even got some compliments—I knew the whole time that it wasn't actually good. It was *done*. There's a difference, and you feel it in your chest when you're delivering something you threw together in a panic versus something you actually had time to think about.

The "I work better under pressure" story is everywhere. The artist who paints a masterpiece the night before the gallery opening. Jimi Hendrix supposedly wrote "Purple Haze" in the dressing room minutes before recording it. These tales get passed around like proof that genius needs urgency.

But here's what those stories almost never mention: the months or years of preparation that came before. Hendrix had been playing guitar for years, had the song structure in his head. The "minutes before recording" part was just the final execution of something that had been brewing for a long time.

When you tell yourself you work better under pressure, you're not comparing pressure-fueled work to calm, steady work. You're comparing it to *nothing*. Because the alternative to working under pressure, in your pattern, isn't working thoughtfully. It's avoiding the work entirely.

Think about Amelia Hayes—an architect who became semi-legendary at her firm for delivering stunning designs exactly 24 hours before every client presentation. Brilliant work. Genuinely beautiful. Her projects won awards. But ask anyone who worked with her and you'd hear a different story.

Her team spent weeks preparing supporting materials, building models, drafting specs, only to receive the actual design at 3 AM the day of the meeting. They'd scramble to integrate everything while Amelia apologized with a charming smile and said she "just needed the pressure to focus."

What nobody saw: the months Amelia spent not working on those projects. The research rabbit holes that led nowhere. The sketches she started and abandoned. She wasn't waiting for pressure to unlock her creativity. She was terrified of committing to a vision, so she delayed until the deadline forced her hand.

And yes, the results were often spectacular. But they were also never *finished*, not really. They were stopped. A finished project has this quality of completion—you explored the possibilities, chose deliberately, arrived somewhere you meant to go. A stopped project just ran out of time.

You might be thinking: but what about genuine cases where pressure produces better results? The game-winning shot in the final seconds, the surgeon who saves a life in a chaotic emergency room?

Fair. But there's a gulf between utilizing adrenaline in an actual emergency and engineering fake emergencies as your standard operating procedure.

A firefighter running into a burning building isn't procrastinating. An ER doctor doing triage isn't avoiding work. They're responding to real urgency with skills they developed through years of consistent, deliberate practice. The pressure is external, unavoidable, and their training kicks in.

When you say you work better under pressure, you're describing something else entirely: a pattern where you manufacture artificial deadlines to replace internal motivation. And the cost of that substitution runs deeper than you probably realize.

The first cost is quality, though not in the obvious way. It's not that pressure-fueled work is always worse—sometimes it's perfectly adequate, occasionally it's even excellent. The problem is you'll never know what you were capable of producing with actual breathing room.

Leo's diorama wasn't terrible. But it also wasn't the project he'd imagined when he first promised Ethan they'd build it together. He'd pictured detailed terrain with real dirt and grass, hand-painted figures, maybe even creative lighting. That vision got sacrificed not because it was impossible, but because he ran out of time. The loss wasn't the grade—it was the gap between what could have been and what actually was.

The second cost is psychological, and it compounds. Joseph Ferrari, a psychologist at DePaul University who's spent decades studying procrastination, calls people like Leo and Amelia "arousal procrastinators." They're not lazy. They genuinely seem to *need* the rush of a looming deadline.

But Ferrari's research suggests this isn't evidence of superior efficiency. It's a specific flavor of procrastination that gets reinforced by the very behavior it drives. The more you succeed under pressure, the more you tell yourself you *need* pressure, and the more you avoid starting anything until pressure arrives. It's a closed loop.

And then there's what psychologists call "self-handicapping"—the tendency to create obstacles to your own success as a way of protecting your ego. If you procrastinate and the work turns out poorly, you can blame the lack of time. You built in an excuse. The pressure myth becomes armor against having to face the possibility that maybe you're not as capable as you think.

I wrote a college essay once at 4 AM after spending an entire weekend doing literally anything else. Got an A-minus. My professor wrote in the margins: "Well-argued but lacks the depth I know you're capable of."

I dismissed it as nitpicking. But here's what bothers me now: I'll never know what that essay could have been. That lost possibility—the version of the work I never got to see—is the real cost.

The third cost is relational, and it radiates outward in ways you don't always notice. When you consistently rely on pressure to function, everyone around you has to absorb your chaos.

Leo's wife Sarah learned to expect the kitchen to transform into a disaster zone whenever a deadline loomed. She stopped making plans for those nights, stopped asking him to help with anything else. His colleagues knew not to count on his input until the absolute last minute. They adjusted. Compensated. Worked around him.

And Ethan—ten years old, watching his dad glue tiny cannons to cardboard at 3 AM—was learning that this is how important things get done. In frantic, exhausting bursts when you've run out of options. The lesson wasn't intentional, but it was loud.

You become someone others have to manage around. And they do it, usually without complaint, because you almost always deliver. But there's a fatigue that builds. A resentment that accumulates. A sense that it doesn't have to be this way but somehow always is.

The fourth cost cuts deepest. Work finished in a rush carries an asterisk that only you can see.

Even when the work gets praised, even when it succeeds by every external measure, there's this nagging awareness that it could have been better. That the compliments are at least partially for effort rather than excellence. That the relief of finishing doesn't quite translate into pride.

David Sedaris wrote *Me Talk Pretty One Day* while working as a house cleaner in Paris, perpetually behind on sleep and rent and everything else. The book launched his career, earned critical acclaim. But when he talks about that period, he doesn't describe creative exhilaration. He describes bone-deep exhaustion. Constant low-grade panic. He wasn't celebrating a preferred working style. He was recounting a survival tactic.

Here's what I've come to understand: the problem isn't that you *can't* produce good work under pressure. It's that you mistake urgency for inspiration. You confuse the tunnel vision that comes from having no other options with the expansive engagement that comes from genuine creative flow.

A friend of mine—I'll call her Rachel—worked as a graphic designer at a mid-sized agency where she built a reputation as the person who could pull off miracles under impossible deadlines. Everyone praised her ability to stay calm and creative even in crisis mode. She got promotions, raises, the best projects.

But when we talked—really talked—she admitted that those "miracles" weren't born from innate talent. They came from years of meticulously avoiding starting anything until she had no choice but to work through the night.

The praise felt hollow because it reinforced a system that left her constantly depleted. What she actually wanted wasn't to be better at crisis management. It was to not need crisis management in the first place.

So she ran an experiment. Started a personal project—a series of illustrations, no client, no deadline. And she committed to working on it for 30 minutes every morning before checking email.

The first week was uncomfortable. She kept reaching for her phone, finding reasons to stop. The work felt slow. Unexciting. Where was the adrenaline rush?

But she kept going. And somewhere around week three, something shifted. The work started building on itself. Ideas from Monday informed Tuesday's session. By Friday she wasn't scrambling to remember what she'd been thinking—she was continuing a conversation she'd started with herself earlier in the week.

What changed was the *experience* of working. Instead of careening between avoidance and panic, she found a sustainable pace. And what disappeared was the constant background hum of anxiety. The knowledge that she was always one missed deadline away from disaster.

Robert Boice, a psychologist who spent decades studying academic writers, discovered something that directly contradicts the pressure myth. Writers who worked in short, regular sessions—even just 30 minutes a day—produced more consistent output and experienced significantly less anxiety than those who waited for long stretches of "free time" before diving into marathon writing sessions.

The steady approach wasn't about superior discipline. It was about building momentum and avoiding the cognitive cost of constantly stopping and restarting. Because when you work in crisis mode, you're not just producing the work. You're also recovering from the depletion of the last crisis and building up anxiety about the next one.

Consistent effort eliminates the recovery tax. You're building on yesterday's progress instead of trying to reconstruct what you were thinking three weeks ago.

So why does the pressure myth persist?

Partly it's narrative. Last-minute rescues and death-defying deadline sprints make compelling stories. We celebrate the hero who saves the day at the eleventh hour, not the person who steadily prevented the crisis from happening in the first place. Quiet consistency doesn't have dramatic tension.

But there's a deeper reason: the pressure myth lets you maintain an illusion of control while sabotaging your own potential.

It's a way of saying "I could have done better if I'd had more time" instead of admitting "Maybe I'm not as capable as I think." Or worse: "Maybe this work scares me and I don't know how to sit with that fear without adrenaline to drown it out."

We engineer artificial urgency because real engagement feels too vulnerable. Too open to judgment. The pressure gives us an out. It protects us from having to fully commit and then potentially fail anyway.

But here's what that protection costs: you never find out what you're actually capable of when you're not operating in survival mode.

Leo sat at his kitchen table at 4:02 AM and let himself feel the full weight of that cost. Not in an abstract way, but as a physical ache in his chest. The diorama would get finished—he always found a way. But this time he didn't mistake the frantic energy for strength. He saw it clearly: a symptom. A signal that something in his relationship to work was fundamentally broken.

He thought about the book he'd been "working on" for two years. The manuscript that existed mostly as scattered notes and half-formed chapters. The story he told himself was that he was waiting for the right stretch of time to really dig in. Some future version of himself with more energy and fewer obligations.

But sitting there, surrounded by glue sticks and miniature soldiers, he recognized that story for what it was: a shield against having to actually do the work and discover whether the book in his head could become the book on the page.

He opened his laptop. Created a new calendar event: 30 minutes, every morning, 6:00-6:30 AM. Just for outlining. Not writing the whole book—just showing up and putting something on the page.

It felt strange. Uncomfortably calm. No urgency, no crisis, no adrenaline telling him this mattered. Just a small, undramatic commitment to doing something before he was desperate.

He didn't know if it would work. But he knew, with sudden clarity, that the alternative—continuing to engineer emergencies and calling it productivity—was eroding something essential. Not just his sleep or his relationships or the quality of his work, but his sense of himself as someone capable of doing hard things without chaos as a prerequisite.

The work you do when you're not in crisis mode might not feel as dramatic. It might not generate the same war stories or the same rush. But it compounds in ways that crisis work never can. Each day builds on the last. Momentum accumulates. And what emerges isn't just better work—it's a different relationship to work entirely.

One where the process becomes sustainable. Where finishing something feels like pride, not just relief. Where you're not constantly borrowing energy from your future self and pretending it's productivity.

The pressure myth promises focus and creativity under the gun. What it delivers is a narrowing of possibilities. A forced march toward completion with no room for exploration, no space for the unexpected connections that emerge when you're not just trying to survive until the deadline.

So here's the question worth sitting with: What would become possible if you stopped engineering emergencies and started trusting that steady, deliberate work could carry you just as far?

Not because you'll suddenly develop superhuman willpower. But because you'll stop spending so much energy managing the chaos you created in the first place. Because you'll give yourself permission to discover what you're actually capable of when you're not just scrambling to survive.

The answer won't reveal itself in a single decision or a burst of motivation. It'll emerge slowly, in the quiet accumulation of days where you showed up without adrenaline forcing you there. Days where you stayed present without panic demanding it. Where you discovered that the work you'd been avoiding wasn't nearly as impossible as the story you'd been telling yourself about needing pressure to handle it.

Leo Maxwell's late-night diorama wasn't just about procrastination; it was about a fundamental miscalculation. He believed pressure would *force* action, but instead found himself locked in a feedback loop of escalating stress and diminishing returns.

# Chapter 5 — The Busy Escape

## Why you can end a full, exhausting day and still not have touched the one thing that mattered

The email from David in accounting sat in Amelia Harper's inbox at 9:47 a.m. on a Tuesday in March. Office supplies. Printer paper, sticky notes, a box of medium-point pens. Nothing urgent. Certainly nothing that required immediate attention. She clicked "approve" anyway.

Amelia approving the office supply request felt good – a quick hit of dopamine, a momentary silencing of that insistent 'monkey.' It wasn't about efficiency; it was about trading genuine progress for immediate relief.

She clicked "approve" anyway.

The Henderson proposal—the one her boss had mentioned last week with that particular combination of casualness and weight that meant *this matters*—remained unopened in a folder on her desktop. Had been sitting there for six days. The proposal that could land the biggest client of the year. The one that would require her to think hard about strategy, to synthesize research, to make an argument she wasn't entirely sure how to construct yet.

But the expense report? That she could finish. Right now. One click.

Done.

The small ping of completion registered somewhere behind her sternum. Not quite satisfaction. More like relief. She'd accomplished something. Checked a box. Made a decision.

Then she opened Slack.

Someone needed to know which conference room was free Thursday. Another person wanted her opinion on font sizes for the quarterly report. A third asked whether the new hires had printer access yet. She answered all of them. Quickly. Efficiently. Each response another tiny checkmark against the growing list of things people needed from her.

Three hours disappeared.

The Henderson proposal sat exactly where she'd left it.

This wasn't laziness—that's the strange part. She hadn't scrolled Instagram or fallen down a YouTube rabbit hole or spent the morning reading news she'd forget by lunch. She'd worked. Steadily. The kind of morning that would look perfectly respectable in any productivity log. Emails answered. Questions fielded. Small fires extinguished.

And yet when the afternoon light started slanting through her office window at that particular angle that meant the day was already half gone, the familiar knot pulled tight in her stomach.

Another day. Another mountain of small tasks conquered.

The one thing that actually mattered? Still untouched.

---

You might be thinking this is just classic procrastination wearing a business casual disguise.

It's not. Not exactly.

The problem isn't choosing distraction over work. It's something stranger and more insidious: a perfectly calibrated system for solving problems you don't actually need to solve in order to avoid facing the one you do.

John Perry, a philosophy professor at Stanford, started noticing this pattern in his own work back in the 1990s. He'd sit down to write a paper—the important one, the one he'd been thinking about for months—and somehow end up reorganizing his bookshelves instead. Or grading papers that weren't due for another week. Or finally dealing with that filing cabinet that had needed attention since 1987.

He wasn't doing nothing. He was accomplishing a tremendous amount. Just never the thing at the top of his list.

He eventually wrote about this in an essay he called "Structured Procrastination," and the central observation was simple but devastating: procrastinators rarely sit idle. They get things done. They're often highly productive people. They just reliably avoid the task that matters most by finding an endless supply of lesser, more manageable alternatives to tackle instead.

The smaller tasks aren't random, either. They cluster around a specific profile: lower stakes, clearer endpoints, less ambiguity, minimal exposure to judgment.

A clean inbox feels good because you can *see* the progress. Zero unread messages. A number that goes down. Your brain registers completion and delivers a small reward.

A large, ambiguous project like crafting a multi-million dollar proposal? No equivalent signal for weeks. Maybe months. You could work on it all day and still have no satisfying sense of *done*. Your brain, wired for immediate rewards and deeply averse to prolonged uncertainty, will steer you toward those quick wins every single time—even when they don't remotely align with what you actually care about.

The rest of your to-do list becomes a menu of perfectly respectable escape routes. And it refreshes daily. Never runs out.

---

I caught myself in this exact trap last fall.

I was supposed to be writing the first draft of a particularly difficult chapter—the one on regret, which felt cosmically appropriate given what I was about to do instead—and I found myself reorganizing my entire file system.

Not because it needed it. Everything was already perfectly functional. I could find any document I needed in under ten seconds.

But I started color-coding folders anyway. Renaming files. Creating nested subdirectories for projects that didn't even exist yet. There was something deeply satisfying about the work. Each folder sliding into place. The clean logic of the hierarchy. The sense that I was *building* something, improving something, making order out of chaos.

Except there was no chaos. Just a chapter I didn't know how to write.

Three days went by before I noticed what I was doing. Three entire days. Solving a problem I absolutely did not have to avoid confronting one I did.

The file system felt *good.* That's the thing. It delivered that little hit of accomplishment with every click. Look at this beautiful structure. Look how organized everything is. You're clearly a person who has their act together.

The chapter? Still a blank page.

The brutal part wasn't the time I'd lost. It was how plausible the whole thing felt while I was doing it. I wasn't lying to myself, exactly. I genuinely believed I was being productive. Responsible, even. Getting my digital house in order before tackling the real work.

But "before" never came.

---

This pattern is particularly corrosive because it doesn't trigger the same guilt response as obvious procrastination. You're not sprawled on the couch watching true crime documentaries at 2 p.m. on a Tuesday. You're *working.* Diligently. Hard. You can account for every minute of your day with perfectly legitimate-sounding explanations.

Which makes it nearly impossible to recognize the problem, let alone fix it.

A wasted day generates a clear signal that something's wrong. A busy day lets the real cost stay hidden.

Sarah Chen figured this out the hard way.

She was a marketing director at a mid-sized tech company in Austin when I first talked to her two years ago. Perpetually swamped. Calendar packed with back-to-back meetings. Known across the company as the person who always responded to emails within an hour. Who could juggle six projects at once without dropping anything.

But when I asked about the launch campaign for their new flagship product—the project that would define her entire year, maybe her whole trajectory at the company—she went quiet for a second.

"I haven't written anything yet," she finally said.

Not a draft. Not an outline. Not even a single strategic document sketching out the vision.

This wasn't incompetence. Sarah was sharp. Capable. Respected by everyone who worked with her.

She was also exquisitely skilled at managing everyone else's priorities while letting her own most important work slip through the cracks.

Every email she answered, every meeting she attended, every minor crisis she defused became an excuse—a perfectly reasonable, defensible excuse—to delay the genuinely daunting task of defining and executing the launch strategy.

Six months later, the product launched with a campaign they cobbled together in three frantic weeks. It wasn't a disaster. It worked well enough. But Sarah knew—and her team knew, and probably her boss knew—that it was nowhere close to what it could have been with six months of real strategic thought behind it.

The knowledge sat there like a stone. This quiet ache of unrealized potential that no amount of busy-work could quite cover up.

---

The danger here isn't just that you're wasting time. It's that you're actively reinforcing the wrong behavior with positive feedback.

Obvious procrastination comes with guilt. An unpleasant but useful signal that something needs to change.

The busy escape generates accomplishment. Sometimes even praise from people around you who can see all the smaller things getting handled so efficiently. Look how responsive she is. Look how much he gets done.

This creates a self-perpetuating loop. You're rewarded for doing more of exactly the thing that doesn't move the needle on your actual goals.

And there's a mechanism underneath this that has to do with how completion *feels* in the brain.

Answering an email gives you closure. Immediate. Measurable. Sent. Done. Off the list. The loop closes.

A large project with high stakes and lots of ambiguity? No such satisfaction for weeks. Maybe months. You could work on it for an entire day and still not have anything you can point to as *finished.*

Your brain isn't wired to wait that long for a reward. It's optimized for survival in an environment where immediate feedback—did I find food, avoid the predator, solve the urgent problem—was the difference between living and dying.

A six-month project with an uncertain outcome and exposure to judgment? That's not the kind of challenge your ancient reward circuitry knows how to handle. It wants the quick win. The clear signal. The thing it can check off and move on from.

So it steers you there. Every single time. Not because you lack discipline. Because your brain is doing exactly what it's designed to do.

---

Then there's the social piece, which makes everything worse.

Small requests from colleagues carry immediate, visible social cost if you ignore them. Someone's waiting on your answer. A client expects feedback. The longer you delay, the more awkward it gets.

The large, personal project you're avoiding? Usually no immediate external pressure. No one's standing over your shoulder asking why you haven't started. The deadline might be weeks away. Or worse—there might not be a hard deadline at all, just this vague sense that you *should* be working on it.

Responding to those external demands feels responsible. Even generous. You're being a good teammate. A reliable colleague.

But it's also a subtle way of letting other people's smaller, louder priorities continually outbid your own larger, quieter ones—every single day—without ever consciously deciding that's the trade you wanted to make.

You become a reactor. Perpetually responding to whatever's most urgent instead of what's most important.

And you might not notice until years have gone by.

---

There's another cost here that's less obvious but maybe more damaging in the long run.

Sophie Leroy, who researches organizational behavior at the University of Washington, discovered something she calls "attention residue" in a series of studies she published in 2009. The basic finding: when you switch from one task to another, part of your attention doesn't make the jump with you. It stays behind, still processing the unfinished business from the previous task.

This isn't just a minor inconvenience. It measurably degrades your performance on whatever you're trying to do next.

Think about what that means for a day built around constant task-switching.

Every time you hop from email to Slack to a quick question from a colleague to a five-minute approval process, you're not just losing the time it takes to handle each thing. You're losing cognitive capacity. Clarity. The ability to think deeply about anything.

You're carrying the mental residue of all those interruptions with you. And it accumulates.

I've felt this in my own work more times than I want to count. After a morning spent answering emails and fielding questions and approving things and weighing in on minor decisions, I'll finally sit down to work on something that requires actual thought—a chapter, a research synthesis, a strategic plan—and it's like trying to run through mud.

My brain won't cooperate. The words don't come. What should take an hour takes three, and even then it doesn't feel quite right.

The work isn't harder because I'm tired. It's harder because I've spent the whole morning training my attention to fragment. And you can't just flip a switch and suddenly think deeply again.

---

Over time, this pattern can reshape how you see yourself.

You might start to believe you're someone who thrives on variety. Who's good at juggling multiple things at once. Who gets energized by a fast-paced, dynamic workload.

And maybe that's true. Some people genuinely prefer that kind of work.

But it's worth testing the belief honestly. Because a genuine preference for variety and an avoidance pattern wearing the same disguise produce identical behavior on the surface—and they require completely different solutions.

Ask yourself: what happens when the important task is actually finished? Does the frantic pace slow down naturally, or do you immediately find new things to fill the space?

The answer tells you whether you're living out a preference or running from discomfort.

---

Benjamin Franklin didn't answer every letter the moment it arrived.

This might seem like a strange historical tangent, but stay with me.

Franklin is famous for his productivity. His output was staggering. Inventor. Writer. Diplomat. Scientist. Printer. Postmaster. He did more in one lifetime than most people could accomplish in three.

But he wasn't frantic. He didn't fill every hour with reactive busyness.

His daily schedule—the one he laid out in his autobiography, the one that's been reproduced in a thousand productivity books since—wasn't about maximizing the sheer volume of activity. It was about deliberately allocating time to what actually mattered.

He carved out specific blocks for work. For reading and improvement. For meals and sleep and what he called "music or diversion or conversation."

The key is what he *didn't* do. He didn't say yes to every request. Didn't attend every social engagement. Didn't let other people's urgent needs dictate how he spent his days.

He understood something that feels almost radical now: saying no to the good is essential for making room for the great.

The busy escape is the opposite of that. It's a relentless yes to everything except the one thing that would actually move your life forward.

And here's what's striking when you read Franklin's letters and diaries: he wasn't naturally disciplined. He struggled with the same pulls toward easier, more immediately gratifying work. He wrote about having to develop specific habits and structures to protect his time because he knew his own inclinations would lead him astray if he didn't.

The difference wasn't some rare internal virtue the rest of us lack. It was that he engineered his environment and routines to make the right choice easy—and the easy escape harder to justify.

---

So what do you actually *do* about this?

Because recognizing the pattern is one thing. Changing it is another.

First: stop treating this like a time management problem.

It's not. You don't need a better calendar system or a new productivity app or a more sophisticated to-do list. The issue isn't that you don't know *how* to prioritize. It's that high-stakes work triggers an emotional response—discomfort, uncertainty, fear of exposure—and your brain is doing what brains do when they detect threat: finding the nearest exit.

The smaller tasks aren't just convenient alternatives. They're relief. A way to feel productive without confronting the thing that's actually making you anxious.

Which means the real work is emotional, not logistical.

You have to build tolerance for the discomfort that comes with important work. And that doesn't happen through willpower. It happens through practice. Through deliberately choosing the hard thing even when—especially when—everything in you wants to reach for something easier.

Start small. Absurdly small if you need to.

If the Henderson proposal feels too overwhelming to start, don't start with the proposal. Start with opening the file. That's it. Just open it. Look at it for thirty seconds. Then close it if you want.

Do that tomorrow. And the day after. Until opening the file doesn't feel like defusing a bomb.

Then extend it. Open the file and read the first paragraph. Or write one sentence. Or sketch a single bullet point.

The goal isn't to finish the project in one heroic session. It's to gradually desensitize yourself to the anxiety that's been keeping you away.

Second: make the escape routes harder to access.

This sounds obvious, but most people don't actually do it. They leave email open all day. Keep Slack notifications on. Let their phone sit on the desk, lighting up with every incoming message.

Every one of those is an open door. An invitation to step away from the hard thing and do something easier instead.

Close the doors.

Turn off notifications. Close your email. Put your phone in another room. Use website blockers if you need to. Make it annoying to check those things during the hours you've set aside for important work.

You're not trying to develop superhuman resistance to distraction. You're trying to make the friction cost of distraction higher than the friction cost of staying focused.

Third: protect specific time for the work that matters.

Not "I'll get to it when I have time." You will never have time. There will always be something else demanding your attention.

Block it on your calendar. Treat it like a meeting you can't move. Two hours. Same time every day if possible. Non-negotiable.

And during those two hours, the only thing you're allowed to work on is the thing you've been avoiding.

If you finish early, great. You can go back to emails and small tasks. But you can't *start* with them. The important work gets first crack at your best cognitive energy, not whatever's left over after you've spent the morning on other people's priorities.

Fourth—and this one's harder—learn to sit with the discomfort of not responding immediately to every request.

The email from David about office supplies? It can wait until the afternoon. The Slack question about conference rooms? Someone else can answer it, or it can sit for an hour.

Nothing catastrophic will happen if you don't respond within ten minutes.

I know it feels that way. The little jolt of social pressure every time you see an unanswered message. The worry that people will think you're unresponsive or difficult or not a team player.

But most of that pressure is self-imposed. And the cost of constantly interrupting your own important work to handle other people's minor requests is far higher than the cost of making someone wait an hour for an answer.

You're not being rude. You're being deliberate about what deserves your attention.

---

Here's what no one tells you about breaking this pattern: it doesn't feel good at first.

The busy escape *works* because it provides relief. Immediate, measurable, socially reinforced relief.

Giving it up means sitting with all the discomfort it was helping you avoid. The uncertainty of the big project. The exposure to judgment. The long stretches of work with no clear finish line in sight.

Your brain will protest. Loudly. It will offer you a thousand perfectly reasonable justifications for why you should just handle this one small thing first. Just clear the decks. Just get organized. Just make sure you're not leaving anyone hanging.

All of it will sound completely sensible.

And all of it will be your brain trying to steer you back toward relief and away from discomfort.

You have to expect this. Prepare for it. Recognize it for what it is when it happens.

It's not evidence that you're doing something wrong. It's evidence that you're doing something hard.

---

The real question isn't whether you can stay busy. You've already proven you can do that.

The question is whether the thing you're busiest with is the thing that actually matters. Whether the work you're pouring your energy into is moving you toward something you care about, or just keeping you occupied enough to avoid the thing you're afraid to face.

And the only way to answer that question honestly is to look at what you've been leaving undone.

Amelia approving the office supply request felt good, a small win in a sea of ambiguity. But that fleeting sense of accomplishment obscured a more unsettling pattern: substituting shallow activity for deep work as if she'd solved a real problem by solving one that barely existed.

# Chapter 6 — The Depleted Chooser

## Why the task you meant to do at 4 p.m. never happens, no matter how much you wanted it to at 8 a.m.

It's 10:47 in the morning, and you're checking your phone at a red light. Email from your boss—needs a quick read, nothing urgent. Text from your partner about dinner plans—you type back "whatever works." Slack notification about a meeting time change—you confirm.

None of this feels like decision-making. It feels like maintenance. Like clearing notifications. But here's what just happened: you made three choices about what deserved your attention, two about how to respond, one about whether to respond at all, and another about whether any of it was urgent enough to delay your left turn. Seven decisions before you've even parked the car. And the workday hasn't started yet.

By 4 p.m., you've made somewhere in the range of hundreds—possibly thousands—of these micro-choices. Not grand strategy. Not life-altering forks in the road. Just the steady hum of: which email first, whether to escalate or smooth over, click this link or skip it, coffee now or later, respond to that comment or let it breathe, attend this optional meeting or buy back the hour. The sheer volume is invisible because each individual choice feels trivial. But trivial is not the same as free.

And then you sit down to do the thing you've been meaning to do all day—the project that actually matters, the one you blocked out time for back when the day looked manageable—and nothing happens. Not because you don't want to do it. You *do* want to do it.

You wanted it at 8 a.m., and you still want it now. But the wanting doesn't translate. You stare at the blank document or the half-finished proposal or the email you need to write, and it's like trying to start a car with a dead battery. The engine of *choosing*—of deciding where to start, what to say first, which angle to take—won't turn over.

And because you can't point to a clear reason it's not happening, you assume the problem is you.

---

I used to think this was a time management issue. That's what most productivity advice assumes: you didn't protect the block, you let other things encroach, you failed to prioritize. And sometimes that's true. But I kept running into people who *had* protected the block. They'd carved out two uninterrupted hours, cleared their calendar, closed their email, done everything the articles said to do—and still couldn't start.

They weren't avoiding the task because it scared them, though that's a real phenomenon we'll come back to. They weren't distracting themselves with something more appealing. They just sat there, stuck, unable to generate momentum. And when I asked them to describe what it felt like, the same word kept coming up: *empty*. Not sad, not anxious. Just out of gas.

That's when I started paying attention to *when* the task was scheduled. And almost every time, it was late. Late morning after a meeting-heavy start. Late afternoon after a day of email triage. Late evening after everything else was handled. The person had done the hard work of clearing space—but they'd cleared it at the end of a long sequence of other decisions, and by the time they arrived at the open space they'd created, they had nothing left to fill it with.

---

The concept that explains this showed up in psychology research in the late 1990s, and it came from a surprising place. Roy Baumeister, a psychologist at Case Western Reserve University, wasn't studying procrastination at all. He was studying self-control—specifically, whether resisting one temptation made it harder to resist another.

The setup was simple. Baumeister brought college students into a lab where chocolate chip cookies were baking. The smell was intentional—warm, distracting, impossible to ignore. He put the cookies on a table in front of them, alongside a bowl of radishes, and split the students into two groups. One group was told they could eat the cookies. The other was told to eat only the radishes—resist the cookies, even though the cookies were right there, still warm, and they were the whole reason the room smelled like a bakery.

Then came the second task: an impossible puzzle. Not hard—actually unsolvable, though the students didn't know that. The question was how long they'd persist before giving up.

The result: students who'd had to resist the cookies gave up on the puzzle faster. Significantly faster. It wasn't that they were less motivated or less intelligent. It was that resisting the cookies had used up something—some internal resource—that they then didn't have available for the puzzle.

Baumeister called it *ego depletion*. The idea was that willpower functioned like a muscle: it could be exercised, but it also fatigued with use. Exert it in one domain, and you'd have less available in another, even if the two tasks were completely unrelated.

The concept caught fire. It fit too well with lived experience to ignore. We'd all felt it—the way a difficult morning made the afternoon feel harder, the way holding your tongue in one meeting made it harder to stay patient in the next. Baumeister's framework gave it a name and a mechanism.

But here's where the science gets messy, and I'm going to pause and tell you this directly because it matters: the original ego depletion findings have not held up cleanly under replication. In the years since Baumeister's initial studies, other researchers have tried to reproduce the effect, and the results have been inconsistent. Some replications worked. Others didn't. There are debates about sample sizes, statistical methods, and whether the effect was ever as robust as it seemed.

So is the whole concept wrong? No. But it's not as simple as "willpower is a fuel tank that empties in a fixed, mechanical way." What's held up better—and what matters more for understanding why you can't start the thing you meant to do at 4 p.m.—is the broader, more specific pattern: *a day full of decisions degrades your willingness and capacity for further decision-making later that same day.*

The mechanism might not be a single depletable resource. It might be a mix of cognitive fatigue, motivational shifts, and an accumulating aversion to the *feeling* of choosing. But the outcome is consistent and observable: your decision-making capacity at 8 a.m. is not the same as your decision-making capacity at 8 p.m., even if nothing particularly dramatic happened in between.

---

The cleanest evidence for this comes from studies of real-world decisions made in sequence. One of the most striking examples:

parole hearings.

Shai Danziger, a researcher in Israel, analyzed over 1,000 parole board decisions made by experienced judges. These weren't hypothetical scenarios in a lab. These were actual rulings that determined whether prisoners would be released or remain incarcerated. High stakes. Serious deliberation. Judges who were trained, professional, and motivated to be fair.

And yet: the likelihood of a favorable ruling dropped dramatically as the session wore on. Early in the morning, judges granted parole about 65% of the time. By late morning, just before a break, that number fell close to zero. After lunch, it spiked back up—and then declined again as the afternoon progressed.

The prisoners whose cases were heard at 9 a.m. and the prisoners whose cases were heard at 4 p.m. weren't systematically different in terms of crime severity, behavior, or rehabilitation. But their outcomes were. The difference wasn't bias in the traditional sense. It was exhaustion. After hours of weighing complex, emotionally demanding decisions, the judges defaulted to the safer, easier option: deny parole. Not because the cases didn't merit release, but because approving release required more cognitive effort than they had left to give.

That's decision fatigue in action. And it's not about willpower or character or how much the judges cared about getting it right. It's about the sheer cumulative weight of choosing, over and over, until the capacity to engage carefully with the next choice simply isn't there anymore.

---

Here's the part that makes this particularly hard to recognize in yourself: decision fatigue doesn't feel like the kind of procrastination you're used to.

When you're avoiding a task because it makes you anxious—because starting it means risking failure, or confronting something uncomfortable, or exposing yourself to judgment—that avoidance has a flavor. You can feel the resistance. You know what you're doing, even if you can't quite stop doing it.

Decision fatigue is quieter. The task doesn't feel bad. You're not actively avoiding it. You're just... not starting. And because there's no obvious emotional resistance to point to, you're left without a good explanation for why it's not happening. That absence of a clear internal story is what makes this form of procrastination so damaging to your self-concept. You can't say "I'm scared of this" or "I'm dreading this," because neither is true. So you default to the only explanation that seems to fit: *I must not be disciplined enough. I must not want it badly enough. I must be lazier than I thought.*

None of that is accurate. But it's the conclusion people arrive at, again and again, because decision fatigue is invisible from the outside and doesn't announce itself from the inside.

---

There's a second layer to this that the psychologist Barry Schwartz uncovered, and it explains why the modern workday is so much more depleting than the volume of *tasks* alone would suggest.

Schwartz studied choice overload—the phenomenon where having *too many options* makes decisions harder, not easier. In one famous study, researchers set up a tasting booth at a grocery store. One day, they offered samples of 24 different jams. Another day, they offered samples of just 6.

The bigger display attracted more attention. But when it came to actual purchases, the smaller display won by a huge margin. The abundance of options didn't empower people to find the perfect jam. It paralyzed them. Evaluating 24 jams was exhausting, and most people walked away without buying anything.

Now think about your workday. Thirty years ago, "send a message" meant write a letter, address an envelope, find a stamp, walk to a mailbox. One method. Today, "send a message" means: email, Slack, text, DM on Twitter, LinkedIn message, WhatsApp, voice memo, video message, or just pick up the phone—and each of those channels has its own norms about urgency, formality, and expected response time. Every message you send now embeds a half-dozen small decisions that didn't used to exist.

The same is true for nearly everything. Lunch used to mean pack a sandwich or go to the diner. Now it means scroll through DoorDash, compare ratings, read reviews, evaluate delivery times, apply promo codes, weigh cost versus quality, and second-guess yourself after you've already ordered. The task—get food—is the same. The number of decisions embedded *in* the task has exploded.

This isn't just about feeling overwhelmed by modern life. It's about understanding that the raw decision load you're carrying on an average Tuesday in 2026 is *structurally heavier* than it was even a decade ago, and certainly heavier than your intuitive sense of "how much a normal day should take out of me" has caught up to reflect.

---

Not all tasks collapse under decision fatigue equally. And understanding why some tasks survive depletion while others don't can change how you structure your day.

A task with a single, pre-determined next step—show up at this address at this time, follow this specific procedure—doesn't require much decision-making *in the moment*. The choosing already happened earlier, when you made the plan. Even if you're tired, you can execute it, because execution is mostly mechanical.

A task with an open, underspecified shape—write something original, have a conversation with no script, solve a problem with no template—requires fresh acts of choosing *at every step*. What angle do I take? What do I say first? What tone fits? How do I structure this? Every one of those is a small decision, and when you're already depleted, each one feels like lifting a weight you don't have the strength for anymore.

This is why "start the proposal" doesn't happen at 4 p.m., but "attend the 4 p.m. meeting" does. The meeting has a fixed start time and a predetermined agenda. You show up, you participate, it ends. The proposal is a blank page and a hundred small choices about what to say and how to say it. One survives depletion. The other doesn't.

I saw this play out with a project manager named Elena, someone I worked with a few years ago. Her mornings were packed with back-to-back check-ins, each one requiring her to assess priorities, troubleshoot blockers, and make quick calls about resource allocation. None of the individual decisions were monumental, but cumulatively they were exhausting. By mid-afternoon, when she'd blocked time to outline the strategy deck her VP had asked for, she couldn't do it. Not because she didn't know the strategy—she knew it cold. But translating that knowledge into a coherent narrative with a logical flow and the right level of detail? That required a kind of active choosing she simply didn't have left. So she'd reorganize her files instead, or respond to non-urgent emails, or schedule more meetings for the following week—tasks that felt productive but didn't require the same generative decision-making. The deck kept getting pushed.

---

The costs of this pattern extend beyond individual missed tasks. There are at least three broader consequences that build quietly over time, and I want to name them directly because they're easy to miss until the damage is done.

**First: you stop trusting your own follow-through.** When a task you genuinely care about keeps not happening, and you don't have a clear explanation for why, the conclusion you draw is almost always about your character, not your capacity. You start to believe you're not disciplined, not committed, not serious. And once that belief sets in, it affects everything. You stop setting ambitious goals because you've internalized the idea that you won't follow through anyway. You preemptively lower your expectations to avoid the disappointment of another failure. The original problem was a timing mismatch—asking your brain to do high-choice work when it had no choices left to give. But the story you tell yourself is much darker, and much more personal.

**Second: decisions made under depletion tend to default to the path of least resistance, which isn't always the same path you'd choose with full capacity.** Agreeing to take on extra work at 9 p.m. because you don't have the energy to negotiate. Saying yes to a commitment you'd normally push back on because saying no would require a longer conversation. Approving a suboptimal solution because exploring better alternatives feels like too much effort. These aren't deliberate choices. They're what happens when the cognitive cost of doing anything *other* than the default option is more than you can pay in that moment. And those defaults accumulate. Over time, they quietly steer your work, your relationships, and your responsibilities in directions you never actively chose.

**Third: important decisions end up getting made at the worst possible time.** If the pattern in your household or your team is that big conversations happen late in the evening—after a full day of work, after the kids are in bed, after everything else has been handled—then the decisions that shape your life are being made in the window when you're *least* equipped to make them well. A career conversation that happens at 10 p.m. on a weeknight is not the same conversation that would happen on a Saturday morning. The participants are the same. The available capacity is not. And the outcome often reflects that, in ways that only become obvious later.

---

Here's the question I know you're asking, because I've asked it myself: what about the people who seem to do their best work under pressure? The ones who claim they're *more* focused, *more* productive when the deadline is closing in?

I don't think they're lying. I think they're mistaking adrenaline for energy.

Urgency can mask depletion. The fight-or-flight response kicks in, cortisol and adrenaline flood your system, and suddenly you're able to push through a task that's been sitting untouched for days. It *feels* like you've found a gear you didn't have before. But you haven't gained capacity—you've just overridden the signal that tells you you're running on empty.

And there's a cost. The work done in that state tends to be lower quality—more reactive, less thoughtful. The recovery time is longer.

And the pattern itself is unsustainable. Relying on urgency to compensate for depletion is like relying on caffeine to compensate for sleep deprivation. It works in the short term. But over time, it just digs the hole deeper.

---

So what do you actually *do* about this?

The first move is simpler than most productivity advice, and it doesn't require a new app or a complicated system: **schedule the task that requires the most original thinking, the most generative decision-making, for the part of the day when you have the most decision-making capacity left.** For most people, that's early. Before the email flood. Before the meetings. Before the hundred small choices that don't feel like choices but are.

This isn't about being a "morning person." It's about basic resource allocation. If you've got a task that's going to require you to make a dozen small creative or strategic decisions—what to emphasize, how to structure it, what tone to take—do it *before* you've spent your decision-making budget on everything else.

I started doing this myself about three years ago, and the difference was immediate. I used to write in the afternoons, after I'd cleared email, handled admin, taken a few calls. It felt responsible—get the urgent stuff out of the way first, then settle into the deep work. But I'd sit down to write and stare at the screen for thirty minutes, deleting and rewriting the same opening sentence. Not because I didn't know what I wanted to say. Because the act of *choosing* what to say first, and how to say it, felt like lifting a piano.

Now I write first. Before I check email. Before I look at Slack. Sometimes before I'm fully awake. And the words come. Not because

I'm more talented in the morning or because I've suddenly developed discipline. Because the part of my brain that makes those micro-choices—this word or that one, this structure or a different one—hasn't been asked to make three hundred other choices yet.

**The second move: reduce the decision load embedded in the task itself.** If the task has an open, underspecified shape, give it more structure *before* the moment you need to execute it. Decide the angle in advance. Outline the sections before you sit down to write them. Break the task into smaller, pre-determined steps so that when you arrive at the task, depleted, there's less left to decide.

This is what checklists do in high-stakes professions. Pilots don't reinvent the pre-flight routine every time they get in the cockpit. Surgeons don't improvise the order of steps in a procedure. The decisions about *what* to do and *in what order* were made once, carefully, and then locked in. Execution still requires skill and focus, but it doesn't require constant choosing.

You can do this with your own work. If you know you'll be depleted by 4 p.m., don't leave "write project update" as a blank, open-ended task. Decide in the morning—when you're sharp—what the three key points are, what order they go in, and what the opening sentence will be. Write those down. Then when 4 p.m. comes and you sit down to write, you're not staring at a blank page trying to generate structure from scratch. You're filling in a framework that already exists.

**The third move: protect the decision-making capacity you do have by ruthlessly eliminating unnecessary choices.** This is what Barack Obama was doing when he wore only gray or blue suits. It's what Steve Jobs was doing with his black turtleneck. They weren't being eccentric. They were conserving cognitive resources for decisions that actually mattered.

You don't have to wear a uniform (though you can—no one's stopping you). But you can ask: which of the small choices I make every day could be automated, batched, or eliminated entirely? What if you ate the same breakfast every weekday? What if you picked out your clothes the night before? What if you processed email twice a day at set times instead of continuously triaging as messages arrived?

Every choice you remove is capacity you get back.

**The fourth move—and this one's harder to implement but possibly the most important—audit where the *important* decisions in your life are actually happening.** If the pattern is that big conversations, strategic planning, or high-stakes negotiations are consistently happening late in the day or late in the week, when everyone involved is already depleted, you're setting those decisions up to fail. Not because the people involved aren't capable, but because you're asking them to bring their best thinking to the moment when they have the least of it available.

Move those conversations earlier. Schedule the budget meeting for Tuesday morning, not Friday afternoon. Have the difficult relationship conversation on a Saturday morning after coffee, not on a Wednesday night after a twelve-hour day. This isn't about convenience. It's about giving the decision the cognitive resources it deserves.

---

There's one more piece to this, and it's about what happens when you *do* miss the task. When 4 p.m. comes, and the thing you meant to do doesn't happen, and you're sitting there feeling like you've failed again.

The story you tell yourself in that moment matters. Not in a self-help, positive-affirmation way. In a practical, functional way. Because if the story you tell yourself is "I'm undisciplined" or "I don't want this enough," that story has consequences. It changes what you try next. It makes you less likely to set ambitious goals, less likely to trust your own intentions, more likely to give up before you start.

But if the story you tell yourself is "I scheduled a high-choice task at the end of a decision-heavy day, and I didn't have the capacity left to do it well"—that's a different story. That story has a fix. That story doesn't indict your character. It just suggests a better time to schedule the task.

The task didn't fail because you're broken. It failed because the design was wrong. And design is fixable.

---

So here's what I want you to try, starting Monday.

Pick one task—the thing you've been meaning to do, the one that keeps sliding to the next day—and ask yourself: how many small decisions does this task actually contain? Not big strategic choices. Small ones. Where to start, what angle to take, what to say first, how to structure it, whether this piece goes here or there.

If the answer is more than a handful, that's a high-choice task. And if you've been trying to do it at the end of the day, after everything else is handled, you've been setting it up to fail.

Tomorrow morning, before you check email, before you do anything else, spend fifteen minutes on it. Not finishing it. Just starting. Making a few of those choices while you still have the capacity to make them well. Decide the structure. Write the opening line. Outline the three main points. Lock in enough of the shape that when you come back to it later—depleted, tired—there's less left to invent and more to simply execute.

And then notice what happens. Not just whether you finish the task, but what it *feels* like to approach it with a full tank versus fumes. Notice whether the task itself feels different. Whether the resistance is still there, or whether what you thought was resistance was just exhaustion wearing a disguise.

Because the thing about decision fatigue is that it's not a character flaw, and it's not a permanent condition. It's a mismatch between the task and the time. And once you see it clearly, once you stop interpreting it as evidence of your inadequacy and start treating it as a design problem—

That's when the task you've been avoiding for weeks finally stops feeling impossible.

And that's when you start to realize: maybe the problem was never *you* at all.

---

It was the *timing*.

Not your discipline. Not your commitment. Not your ability to follow through. The timing was wrong, and because you didn't know that timing mattered—because you thought willpower was supposed to be a constant, a renewable resource you could summon on demand—you kept trying to force the square peg of a high-stakes decision into the round hole of a depleted afternoon.

And when it didn't fit, you blamed the peg.

But here's what changes when you start treating decision fatigue as a design problem instead of a moral one: you stop scheduling cognitively demanding tasks for cognitively bankrupt hours. You stop putting "make a hard decision" on your to-do list for 7 p.m. on a Wednesday after a day full of meetings, emails, and minor choices that felt minor but weren't. You stop acting as if your 4 p.m. self has the same resources as your 9 a.m. self, because they don't.

They're working with different operating systems. One is running on a full charge. The other is in low-power mode, dimming the screen and shutting down background apps just to stay functional.

And once you see that—once you accept that your cognitive capacity fluctuates across the day the same way your energy does—you start making different choices. Not harder ones. Different ones.

You move the intimidating task to the morning, before the inbox floods and the Slack notifications start stacking. You batch the small decisions so they don't bleed across the entire day. You notice which decisions you can automate or eliminate entirely, not because you're lazy, but because you're strategic. Because you've realized that every trivial choice you *don't* have to make is capacity you're saving for something that matters.

You start to understand that the people who seem to have endless willpower aren't necessarily stronger than you. They've just—consciously or not—structured their lives to protect their decision-making reserves. They wear the same thing every day. They eat the same breakfast. They don't browse twenty options when two will do. Not because they lack imagination, but because they've done the math: every choice costs something, and they'd rather spend that cost on choices that count.

This isn't about rigidity. It's about recognition. It's about seeing that your attention and your willpower are *finite*, and that pretending otherwise doesn't make you virtuous—it just makes you tired.

And it's about noticing the quiet cruelty of a culture that pretends otherwise. That sells you the idea that if you just wanted it badly enough, you'd find a way. That treats depletion as a symptom of insufficient motivation rather than a predictable consequence of being a human being navigating a world designed to exhaust you.

Because the truth is, you *do* want it. You wanted it at 8 a.m., and you still want it at 4 p.m. The wanting hasn't changed. What's changed is your capacity to act on it. And mistaking one for the other—mistaking a resource problem for a commitment problem—is how you end up in a cycle of self-blame that has nothing to do with what's actually happening.

So what *is* actually happening?

You're encountering the same thing every person encounters when they run a system past its design limits. You're trying to make decisions with a decision-maker that's offline. You're asking your prefrontal cortex to do complex cost-benefit analysis when it's already spent the day adjudicating whether to respond to that email now or later, whether to order salad or pasta, whether to take the call or let it go to voicemail.

Individually, none of those choices feel significant. Collectively, they add up. And by the time you get to the task that *actually* matters—the one you told yourself you'd handle at 4 p.m.—there's nothing left in the tank.

Not because you're weak. Because you're human.

And humans, it turns out, are not designed to make three hundred decisions a day and still have the clarity to make one more. We're designed to make a handful of good ones, and then rest. We're designed to protect our cognitive resources, not spend them on things that don't matter. We're designed to notice when we're running low and adjust accordingly.

But we've been taught to override that signal. To push through. To treat exhaustion as a challenge to conquer rather than information to respect.

And that's the shift.

When you stop treating your 4 p.m. resistance as a test of character and start treating it as data—as your system telling you it's tapped out, that it needs a different approach or a different time—you stop fighting yourself.

You stop trying to prove you can do the hard thing when you're already running on empty.

And you start designing a life that works *with* your capacity, not against it.

Because the goal was never to be superhuman.

It was to stop mistaking depletion for failure, and to start recognizing that the version of you at 8 a.m. and the version of you at 4 p.m. are both *you*—just operating under different constraints.

And once you see that clearly, the task doesn't have to feel impossible anymore.

It just has to be scheduled for a time when you actually have what it takes to do it.

By 10:47 AM, that initial reservoir of choice had already been significantly drained, leaving less and less capacity for anything requiring real effort.

What drained it?

Not the big choices. Not the dramatic moments of willpower. But the accumulated weight of a hundred small decisions that individually seemed like nothing at all.

Whether to answer that email now or later. Which shirt to wear. Whether the meeting really needed to happen or could wait. What to eat for breakfast. Whether to push back on that request or just say yes. Whether to check your phone. Whether to open the browser tab that just caught your eye. Whether to care about the thing you're supposed to care about right now, or let it slide.

Every single one of those moments—no matter how trivial—required your brain to evaluate options, weigh consequences, override an impulse, and commit to a direction.

And every single one cost you something.

The researcher Roy Baumeister, who pioneered much of the work on ego depletion, demonstrated this with disarming simplicity. In one study, participants were asked to resist eating freshly baked cookies placed in front of them, while others were allowed to eat freely. Afterward, both groups were given an impossible puzzle to solve. The cookie-resisters gave up significantly faster. Not because they were less intelligent or less motivated—but because resisting the cookies had quietly depleted the same mental resource they needed to persist on the puzzle.

The mechanism wasn't moral. It was metabolic.

Your prefrontal cortex—the part of your brain responsible for executive function, impulse control, and deliberate choice—runs on glucose. And while your brain represents only about two percent of your body weight, it consumes roughly twenty percent of your energy. When you make decisions, inhibit urges, or regulate your emotions, that energy expenditure spikes. And as the day wears on and those micro-expenditures accumulate, the fuel runs low.

Which means that by the time 4 p.m. rolls around, the version of you sitting at your desk is neurologically not the same person who set the intention at 8 a.m.

You haven't become lazy. You haven't lost your values. You haven't suddenly stopped caring about the goals you set for yourself.

You've just run out of the biological substrate that makes effortful choice possible.

And here's the part that makes it worse: the depletion doesn't announce itself. You don't get a notification on your phone that says, "Warning: executive function at 34% capacity." You just notice that the thing you were supposed to do feels harder than it should. That the email you meant to write seems more draining than it did this morning. That the boundary you planned to hold suddenly feels too exhausting to defend.

And because you don't recognize the depletion for what it is, you interpret it as a referendum on your character.

You tell yourself you're procrastinating. That you lack discipline. That if you really wanted it, you'd find a way.

But the truth is simpler and far less personal: you're trying to run software on hardware that no longer has the power to execute it.

The implications of this are both humbling and liberating.

Humbling, because it means you are not, in fact, in full control of your behavior at all times. You are subject to constraints you can't willpower your way past. There are hours of the day when certain tasks are functionally out of reach, not because you're weak, but because the system has limits.

Liberating, because once you accept that, you stop wasting energy on self-recrimination and start designing around the constraint instead.

You stop scheduling your hardest creative work for late afternoon, when your capacity for deep focus has already been carved away by a dozen small decisions. You stop putting difficult conversations at the end of a long day, when your ability to regulate emotion and hold nuance is at its lowest. You stop assuming that if you just tried harder, you could override the biology.

And you start treating your decision-making capacity the way you'd treat any other finite resource: as something to conserve, allocate strategically, and replenish when possible.

This doesn't mean you're off the hook. It doesn't mean effort doesn't matter, or that discipline is irrelevant. It means you stop applying effort in ways that ignore how the system actually works.

Because here's what happens when you do ignore it:

You set an intention in the morning—maybe to go to the gym after work, or to finally have that hard conversation with your partner, or to spend an hour on the project that actually matters—and you mean it. You genuinely believe you'll follow through. And then the day unfolds. A conflict at work. A tedious meeting that required you to stay patient when you wanted to snap. A decision about whether to take on one more thing. Another decision about how to respond to a passive-aggressive email. Another about whether to eat the thing you're craving or the thing you're supposed to want.

By the time 4 p.m. arrives, you're still you. But the version of you that shows up has already spent the currency required to do the hard thing.

And so you don't do it.

Not because you're weak. Not because the goal didn't matter. But because the system that enables hard choices had already been depleted before you even got to the choice that counted most.

The pattern repeats. The goal gets deferred. And over time, you start to believe a story about yourself: that you're the kind of person who doesn't follow through. That you lack the willpower to do what you say you'll do. That there's something fundamentally broken in your character.

But the real problem isn't your character.

It's that you've been trying to make important decisions at the point in the day when you have the least capacity to make them.

And once you see that, the solution isn't to try harder.

It's to stop scheduling the things that require the most from you at the times when you have the least to give.

It's to recognize that willpower isn't a fixed trait you either have or don't have—it's a depletable resource that fluctuates predictably over the course of a day.

And it's to start building a life that acknowledges that reality, instead of one that pretends you're supposed to be equally capable at all hours.

Because you're not.

And you were never supposed to be.

By 10:47 AM, seven seemingly insignificant decisions had subtly depleted her mental resources. The cumulative effect of these micro-choices reveals how easily we can sabotage ourselves before ever reaching the task that truly matters.

# Chapter 7 — The Verdict You're Avoiding

## Why the manuscript never gets sent, and the email never gets opened

Harper Lee never published another novel after *To Kill a Mockingbird.* Not because she lacked talent or ambition, but because the act of finishing felt…dangerous. The weight of expectation, the fear of failing to recapture lightning in a bottle, proved more paralyzing than any writer's block.

The chipped Formica countertop served as a constant reminder of the unfinished tasks, a silent witness to the emotional weight she carried. It wasn't just a surface; it was a symbol of her internal resistance – and a place where avoidance had become deeply ingrained.

But here's what's strange about that explanation: it assumes the problem was *ambition*, when everything about her pattern suggests it was something else entirely. Because if you wanted to write something new, something different, you'd... write it and send it out. The issue wasn't whether people would compare it to *Mockingbird.* The issue was that Lee would know—before anyone else did—whether it measured up. And as long as those pages stayed in the drawer, they existed in a kind of liminal space. Potentially brilliant. Possibly career-defining. Certainly *something.*

The moment she mailed them off, that possibility would collapse into a single, fixed verdict.

This is the species of procrastination that doesn't announce itself with obvious chaos. Your house isn't a mess. Your email inbox isn't exploding. You're not missing meetings or forgetting to pay bills.

From the outside, you look fine. Productive, even. But there's this one thing—this manuscript, this conversation, this question you could ask—that sits at the edge of your awareness, quietly gathering weight. It's not that you don't have time. It's that every time you think about doing it, something in your chest tightens, and you find a reason to do literally anything else.

The email you haven't opened for three weeks isn't complicated. It's probably feedback from your manager, or test results from your doctor, or a response from someone whose opinion you value. Opening it would take eleven seconds. But you don't. Because you already know—not *know* know, but sense in some pre-verbal way—that the information inside will change how you see yourself. Maybe it'll confirm something you've been afraid is true. Maybe it'll force you to make a decision you've been avoiding. Either way, the act of *not* opening it keeps the future suspended, unresolved, still negotiable.

I did this once with something that should have been straightforward. I had three weeks to pitch for a speaking opportunity I'd wanted for years—one of those invitations that felt like a door opening to exactly the kind of work I'd imagined doing. The brief was clear. I had the expertise. And for the first two weeks, I was *busy*. I reorganized my portfolio. I studied other people's decks, took notes on what worked, what didn't. I revised my bio four times. Useful work, technically. Productive, even.

By week three, the actual pitch document was still blank. And the more time passed, the higher the stakes felt. Because now it wasn't just "Will this pitch be good enough?"—it was "Why did I wait so long? What does it say about me that I'm cutting it this close?" The delay had generated its own separate problem. And when the deadline arrived, I looked at the empty document and told myself I wasn't ready. That I needed more time to make it really strong. That sending something half-baked would be worse than not sending anything at all.

Someone else got the spot. And I got to keep my story about what *could* have happened, if only I'd had a little more time.

Here's the thing that makes this pattern so slippery: the avoidance feels rational in the moment. You're not being lazy. You're being *careful*. Thoughtful. Waiting for the right conditions. But if you actually look at what you're protecting yourself from, it's not failure in the task—it's exposure of something you're afraid might be true about you. The manuscript isn't just a stack of pages. It's a test of whether you're actually a writer, or just someone who likes the idea of being one. The application isn't just paperwork. It's a referendum on whether you belong in that room, whether you're as capable as you've told yourself you are.

And the brilliance—if you can call it that—of leaving it undone is that you never have to find out.

There's a reason this doesn't feel like ordinary procrastination. When you're avoiding doing the dishes, you know exactly what the problem is: dishes are boring and your hands will smell like old food. The task itself is the obstacle. But when you're staring at a finished draft you won't send, or a voicemail you won't listen to, or a conversation you won't initiate, the difficulty isn't in the doing. You could do it right now. You could finish it in the time it takes to read this paragraph.

What you're actually avoiding is *knowing*.

A friend of mine—let's call her Maya—spent eight months applying to graduate programs. She researched schools, requested transcripts, asked for recommendation letters, wrote and rewrote her personal statement until it was sharp and clear and true. Every piece of the application was ready. And then, one by one, the deadlines passed. She didn't submit. Not because she forgot—she had calendar reminders, sticky notes, friends checking in. She just... didn't do it. When I asked her why, she said something that stuck with me: "As long as I didn't apply, I could still believe I'd get in."

That sentence is the whole pattern in miniature.

Because here's what happens when you actually submit the thing, open the email, ask the question: you get an answer. And answers are fixed. Definite. A rejection isn't a theoretical possibility anymore—it's a fact you have to carry. But if you never submit, never ask, never open the envelope, the outcome stays fluid. You can still be the person who *would have* succeeded, if only circumstances had been different. If only you'd had more time. If only the timing had been better.

It's a perfect defense, except for one problem: your life doesn't move forward.

You know what's worse than getting a rejection? Spending five years not knowing. Because the not-knowing doesn't stay neutral. It curdles. What starts as "I'm waiting for the right moment" becomes "I don't think I'm good enough" becomes "People like me don't do things like that." The thing you were protecting—your sense of competence, your potential, your belief in yourself—slowly erodes anyway, not because you failed, but because you never tried.

I see this sometimes in people who are brilliant at their jobs but mysteriously terrible at asking for raises. They'll prepare for weeks. Make spreadsheets of comparable salaries, rehearse their pitch, gather documentation of their contributions. And then the meeting with their manager comes and goes, and they don't bring it up. Afterward, if you ask what happened, they'll say the timing didn't feel right, or their boss seemed stressed, or they didn't want to seem greedy. But if you dig a little, what you find underneath is this: asking for more money means claiming you're *worth* more money. And if your manager says no—or worse, seems surprised you'd even ask—that's not just a professional setback. It's a kind of verdict on your value as a person.

Easier not to ask. Easier to stay in the realm of "I could have, but I didn't" than to risk landing in "I asked, and they said no."

The cruelest part of this is how it compounds. Because the thing you're avoiding doesn't just sit there neutrally. It grows. A manuscript unsent for a month carries the fear of rejection. A manuscript unsent for a year carries that *plus* the fear of what your delay says about you—your discipline, your seriousness, your belief in your own work. An email unopened for a week is just an email. An email unopened for six months is a symbol of everything you'd rather not confront. The avoidance creates its own separate layer of shame, which makes the task even harder to face, which makes you avoid it longer, which generates more shame.

You end up trapped in a loop where the only thing worse than facing the verdict is facing why you've been avoiding it for so long.

Here's what this costs, in concrete terms. Not in some abstract sense of "missed opportunities," but in the actual texture of your days. You wake up and the thing is there, waiting. You check your email and see the message you still haven't opened, the reply you still haven't sent. You sit down to work and the task you're avoiding hums in the background, pulling a steady trickle of your attention even when you're focused on something else. It's not that you're thinking about it constantly—it's worse than that. It's always *almost* in your thoughts, a low-grade noise you can never quite tune out.

And because you can't resolve it—because resolving it would mean facing the thing you're afraid to face—you develop elaborate workarounds. You throw yourself into other projects. You stay busy in ways that feel productive but don't actually move your life forward. You get very good at looking like you're making progress while avoiding the one thing that would actually change something.

Meanwhile, weeks pass. Then months. Then years.

You might be thinking this is overstating it. That comparing an unopened email to some kind of existential crisis is dramatic. And sure, maybe. But pay attention to how it feels in your body when you think about doing the thing you've been avoiding. Not the story you tell yourself about why you haven't done it yet—the actual physical sensation. Is your chest tight? Is your breathing shallow? Are you suddenly aware of seventeen other things you could be doing instead?

That's not nothing. That's your entire nervous system trying to protect you from a threat it perceives as real.

The problem is, the threat isn't real. Or rather—it's real in the sense that you might get bad news, might face criticism, might discover something uncomfortable. But it's not dangerous. No one's physical safety depends on whether you open that email or send that manuscript or ask that question. The part of you that's running this avoidance protocol is using the same alarm system that kept your ancestors alive when predators were an actual daily concern. Except now it's firing in response to... feedback on a draft. A performance review. Someone's opinion of your work.

The system can't tell the difference. To the ancient, self-protective part of your brain, social rejection registers the same way a physical threat does. And so you avoid, because avoidance feels like survival.

But here's the thing about survival: you're already surviving. The question is whether you're also *living*.

There's a version of you that exists on the other side of the thing you're avoiding. That version has information you don't have. They know how the pitch was received, what the test results were, whether the person said yes or no. And here's what's strange: that version of you is almost always better off than the current version, even if the news is bad. Because they're not carrying the weight of the unknown anymore. They're not organizing their entire life around avoiding a single piece of information. They've faced the thing, survived it, and moved on.

The version of you on this side—the one still avoiding—is stuck. Not because the task is hard. Because the verdict feels too important to risk.

So what's the way through? Not around, not over—*through*. And it starts with something simpler than you'd think: separating the outcome from your worth.

Write it down. Actually write it. "If this pitch is rejected, it means..." and then finish the sentence with what it actually means, not what it *feels* like it means. A rejected pitch means that specific opportunity didn't work out. It doesn't mean you're not a good speaker, or that you'll never get another chance, or that you were foolish to want it in the first place. Those are stories you're adding. The actual, factual meaning of a rejection is just: not this one, not this time.

Once you've written that down—once you've named the actual stakes instead of the catastrophic imagined ones—the next step is to shrink the window. Because the danger zone isn't the doing, it's the *almost* doing. That gap between "essentially ready" and "actually sent" is where the avoidance thrives. So make the gap small. Tell someone you'll submit by Friday and ask them to check in. Schedule the appointment and put it in your calendar with reminders. Create a structure where not doing it has a social cost that outweighs the emotional cost of doing it.

And then—this is the part that matters—reframe the goal. The goal isn't "get accepted." The goal is "collect real information." Because here's the truth: you don't actually know what will happen until you try. All the worrying, all the imagined outcomes, all the rehearsed worst-case scenarios—they're just guesses. You're avoiding a guess. The only way to trade the guess for actual information is to do the thing.

Maybe it goes badly. Maybe the feedback is harsh, or the answer is no, or the conversation is harder than you hoped. That's real information. You can work with it. You can revise, try again, adjust your approach, learn something. What you can't do—what no one can do—is grow while staying in the realm of "what if."

The verdict you're avoiding isn't out there waiting for you. It's already here, in the space between where you are and where you're trying to go. And the only way to dissolve it is to stop treating it like a judgment and start treating it like data.

You're not protecting yourself by waiting. You're just choosing a different kind of pain—the slow, compounding ache of wondering what might have been, instead of the sharp, clean hurt of knowing what is.

Harper Lee's unpublished manuscripts aren't simply stories left unfinished; they are physical manifestations of a particular kind of internal conflict. Her avoidance wasn't about lacking talent, but rather confronting a hidden verdict she refused to deliver.

# Chapter 8 — The Line Between Won't and Can't

## Why "just start" is sometimes exactly the right advice, and sometimes cruel

Amelia had been sitting at her kitchen table for forty-seven minutes. The medical bills were still in their envelopes, still arranged in that careful pile she'd made when she first sat down with her coffee—which had gone cold an hour ago, the ceramic mug leaving a ring on the Formica. She wasn't afraid of what the bills contained; she was stuck in the *space* between knowing and doing.

She found herself endlessly rearranging the medical bills, sorting them by date, then amount, then insurance provider. It wasn't about understanding the charges; it was about recreating a sense of control, a familiar pattern of meticulous preparation that had once served her well – but now only trapped her further.

Her hand would reach for the top envelope, pause, withdraw. Reach again. Pause. She'd rearrange the stack—smallest to largest, then chronological, then back to smallest again. She wasn't afraid of what she'd find. She wasn't avoiding bad news. She just...couldn't make the first action happen.

Across town, Leo had been staring at a blank Word document for two hours. The cursor blinked at him, patient and accusing. He had a 47-page outline pinned above his desk. Character sketches. Plot points color-coded in a spreadsheet. He'd been planning this novel for eight months. He *wanted* to write it—genuinely, desperately. He could see the opening scene: a woman on a train platform in winter, her breath visible, a suitcase at her feet. He knew what she was wearing. He knew what she was thinking. He knew the first line of dialogue.

He could not type the first sentence.

Not because he feared it would be bad. Not because he was waiting for the perfect opening. His fingers hovered over the keys, and the signal from his brain—the one that should say *start typing now*—just dissipated somewhere between intention and action.

For most of this book, we've been talking about people like Amelia and Leo as if they're stuck for the same reason: a task provokes a negative feeling, the mind escapes it, and the solution is to change the terms or shrink the threat until starting becomes possible. That's true for most procrastination. Maybe even the vast majority. But this chapter exists because there's a second kind of stall that looks identical from the outside, responds to none of those fixes, and gets misdiagnosed so often that people spend *years* believing something is fundamentally wrong with their character when the actual issue is something else entirely.

The distinction comes down to whether the blockage is primarily *emotional* or primarily *mechanical*. Emotional avoidance is what we've been discussing: you freeze on the manuscript because you're afraid it won't be good enough, or you delay the conversation because you dread conflict, or you can't open the bills because facing what's inside feels overwhelming. The stall is a defense mechanism. Those situations respond to structural overrides: smaller steps, lower stakes, external scaffolding, identity reframes. You change the shape of the threat, and the avoidance loosens.

But some people—and some tasks, even for people without any diagnosed condition—hit a wall that isn't emotional at all. The difficulty is with what psychologists call *executive function*: the brain's ability to plan, initiate, sustain, and shift attention across a task. Think of it as air traffic control for your actions. It takes "I need to start the grant application" and translates it into the sequence of steps required to open your laptop, find the file, read the first question, type a response. When that system works smoothly, you barely notice it. When it doesn't, you get Leo sitting at his desk for two hours, wanting to write, knowing what to write, and unable to make his fingers move.

Russell Barkley, who has spent decades studying ADHD, argues that it's not a disorder of *knowledge*—it's a disorder of *performance*. People with ADHD don't fail to understand what they should do, or when, or why. They fail to mobilize the cognitive resources required to actually *do* it at the moment it needs to happen. The gap isn't between ignorance and understanding; it's between understanding and action. And that gap is invisible from the outside, which is why it gets mistaken for laziness, lack of discipline, or—most cruelly—not caring enough.

(You might be thinking: "I don't have ADHD, so this doesn't apply to me." Maybe. But executive function exists on a spectrum, and it can be situationally impaired even in people with no diagnosable condition. Chronic stress, sleep deprivation, depression, decision fatigue—these all degrade executive function temporarily. And some people simply have less robust executive function as a baseline trait, the way some have worse eyesight. It's not a character issue. It's a capacity issue.)

The trouble is that these two situations—emotional avoidance and executive function difficulty—produce nearly identical outward symptoms. An unstarted task. A person who can't explain why they can't begin. A history of missed deadlines despite expressed intentions. From the outside, and often from the inside, they look the same. Which means people get the wrong diagnosis, apply the wrong fix, and conclude the real problem is willpower when it may not be a willpower problem at all.

Let me give you a real example.

In 2004, Martha Stewart went to prison. Not for insider trading—she was never convicted of that—but for obstruction of justice and lying to investigators. The case centered on her sale of ImClone stock in 2001, which happened just before the stock price tanked. The SEC opened an investigation. And here's where it gets interesting: by all accounts, Stewart didn't refuse to cooperate because she was guilty, or because she thought herself above the law. Witnesses described something stranger—an almost inexplicable paralysis around providing documentation, returning phone calls, responding to straightforward requests. She'd agree to do something, then simply…not do it. Not defiantly. Just…not.

Her lawyers were baffled. Prosecutors took it as evidence of guilt. But people close to her described a pattern they'd seen before: when faced with tasks requiring administrative follow-through—especially tasks she found tedious or beneath her skill level—Stewart would freeze. Not avoid. *Freeze.* She'd acknowledge the need, express intent, and then be genuinely unable to make herself execute the boring, repetitive steps required. It wasn't malice. It was a cognitive jam, one that her obsessive perfectionism and relentless work ethic in other domains had mostly masked until it suddenly, catastrophically, mattered.

I'm not diagnosing Martha Stewart. I'm pointing out that the woman who built a billion-dollar empire on meticulous attention to detail could, in certain contexts, be genuinely unable to complete straightforward administrative tasks—and that inability didn't stem from not caring. It stemmed from something else. Something that looked, from the outside, like stubbornness or contempt, but was actually a specific difficulty with initiation and follow-through on tasks that didn't engage her in the right way.

That's the shape of executive function difficulty: uneven, context-dependent, baffling to observers, and often layered with shame, because the person experiencing it can't make sense of why they can do enormously difficult things in one domain and completely fail at objectively simpler things in another.

So how do you tell the difference?

There are clues. Honest, imperfect clues—not a diagnostic checklist—but enough to point you in the right direction.

**First: selectivity.** Emotional avoidance tends to be task-specific. You freeze on the thing that triggers fear or discomfort, but you can start other difficult tasks without much trouble. The person who can't open the email from their boss can still tackle a complex work project, organize a party, or deep-clean the garage. The avoidance maps onto the emotional content, not the difficulty level.

Executive function difficulty is less selective. It shows up across multiple contexts, including ones you genuinely *want* to do. The novelist who can't start the book he's been planning can also struggle to start errands, emails, simple household tasks. The pattern isn't "I freeze on things I'm afraid of"; it's "I freeze on things requiring sustained self-directed initiation, regardless of how much I want them."

**Second: the presence or absence of a nameable fear.** If you ask someone avoiding a task why they're stuck, they can usually tell you. They're afraid of criticism, or failure, or confronting how far behind they've gotten. The fear might be irrational or hard to shake—but it's *there*, and they can name it.

If you ask someone with genuine initiation difficulty why they're stuck, they often struggle to articulate anything specific. It's not evasiveness. There genuinely isn't a feared outcome driving the freeze. They *want* to do the task. They don't feel afraid. And yet they cannot make the sequence of decisions and actions actually *happen.* That absence—the lack of a story about what bad thing will happen—is itself diagnostic.

I talked to a woman named Rachel a few years ago who'd been trying to write her dissertation for three years. She loved her topic. She had tenure-track offers waiting. She had no fear of defending her work; she'd presented chapters at conferences to positive reception. But every time she sat down to write, she'd open the document, read what she'd written, and then…just sit there. She described it as a wall of static between her thoughts and her fingers. She could think the sentences. She could say them out loud. She could not type them. There was no fear to name. No perfectionism to unpack. Just a strange, maddening inability to translate intention into action.

Rachel eventually got evaluated for ADHD—something she'd never considered because she'd been a straight-A student—and was diagnosed in her early thirties. The difficulty wasn't motivation. It was a specific impairment in the brain's ability to initiate and sustain effortful, self-directed tasks, especially ones without external deadlines or built-in accountability. Once she had the right frame, she stopped trying to force herself through willpower and started building external scaffolding: body-doubling with a friend who'd work silently in the same room, breaking chapters into absurdly small daily targets, using a timer to create artificial urgency. She finished the dissertation in four months.

If you treat genuine executive function difficulty as ordinary emotional avoidance, you end up giving advice that doesn't just fail—it actively *harms*. "Just start." "Try harder." "You're not wanting it enough." Those exhortations land on someone who is already trying, already wanting it, already baffled by their inability to act—and they confirm the worst story that person tells themselves, which is that something is fundamentally broken in their character. Years of this. Years of effort aimed at the wrong target. Years of believing you're weak-willed when the actual issue is a specific, nameable neurological difference that responds to structure, not shame.

And the relational cost compounds it. A partner watching you fail to start the same task over and over draws conclusions: you don't care, you're not trying, you're lazy. A manager who sees you miss deadlines despite expressed commitment questions your reliability. Those judgments land on top of the original difficulty and create a second layer of harm—because now you're not just struggling to start things, you're also managing other people's disappointment and mistrust.

The reverse is also true. If you treat emotional avoidance as an unchangeable capacity limit, you foreclose real progress. "I just can't start things" becomes an identity, a fixed story about how you're wired, and you stop trying interventions that might actually work.

Getting the diagnosis right isn't an intellectual exercise. It's the difference between years of effort in the wrong direction and a much shorter path to support that actually fits.

There's a shadow category worth naming: difficulty initiating action that comes with clinical depression, chronic fatigue, or other whole-system conditions. A person in a depressive episode might genuinely *want* to do things, understand why they matter, and still find initiating almost *any* effortful action nearly impossible—not because of task content, and not because of a specific executive function impairment, but because of a generalized depletion affecting everything at once. That's a different animal, and it requires clinical intervention, not productivity hacks.

I can describe these distinctions. I can offer a framework for thinking them through. But I can't diagnose you, and this chapter isn't a substitute for professional assessment. Some of you will finish this chapter with clarity. Some with reasonable suspicion. And if you're in the second group, the honest next step isn't more self-analysis—it's a conversation with someone qualified to help you sort it out properly.

Because here's the thing: if the issue is genuine executive function difficulty, the solution isn't willpower. It's structure. External scaffolding. Accommodation. The same way you wouldn't tell someone with poor eyesight to "just try harder" to see the whiteboard, you don't tell someone with impaired initiation capacity to "just start." You give them glasses. You change the environment to fit the constraint.

What does that look like in practice?

**Breaking tasks into smaller units**—sometimes absurdly small. Not because you're incapable of understanding the larger goal, but because each decision point requires cognitive effort, and reducing decision points per session makes initiation more achievable. Instead of "write the chapter," it's "open the document." That's the whole task for today. Tomorrow, "write one paragraph." Not as a motivational trick—as an accommodation.

**Creating external accountability.** Not because you don't care about the outcome, but because external deadlines and other people's expectations provide the scaffolding that your internal executive function doesn't reliably generate. This is why some people can't write the novel but can meet every work deadline: the work deadline comes with external structure built in.

**Body-doubling:** working in the same space as someone else, even if they're doing something completely unrelated. It sounds almost magical until you try it and realize that the mere presence of another person working creates a kind of borrowed focus, a scaffolding that makes staying on task easier. It's not about accountability—they're not watching you—it's about reducing the cognitive load required to sustain attention.

**Visual cues and checklists.** Not because you'll forget what to do, but because externalizing the sequence of steps removes one layer of cognitive demand. You're not holding the plan in working memory while also trying to execute it; you're offloading the plan onto paper, which frees up capacity for execution.

**Using timers to create artificial urgency.** The Pomodoro Technique—25 minutes of focused work, 5-minute break—works for many people not because it's motivating but because it creates a clear, bounded window of effort. You're not committing to finishing the whole project; you're committing to 25 minutes. That smaller commitment is easier to initiate, and once you're in motion, continuing often becomes easier than starting was.

None of these are willpower solutions. They're structural accommodations, the same way a ramp is an accommodation for someone who can't use stairs. And if you need them, there's no shame in that—though I know the culture tells you otherwise, tells you that needing external scaffolding means you're not disciplined enough. That story is wrong. It's also cruel. And it keeps people stuck for years in a pattern they could exit if they had the right support.

Amelia rearranging medical bills felt strangely…productive. But it was an illusion of control, a way to feel like she was *doing* something without actually facing the underlying issue—a distinction that's critical for understanding why 'just start' often fails so spectacularly.

# Chapter 9 — The Vague Task

## Why "clean the garage" never happens, and "put the three boxes by the door in the car" does

The chipped Formica countertop held the weight of everything Amelia hadn't done. Not literally—it wasn't supporting a stack of unfinished paintings or unwritten novels. Just a ceramic fruit bowl, overflowing with oranges and grapefruits she'd bought two weeks ago in a burst of optimism that now felt almost comical.

Her husband David walked in, grabbed a mug from the rack. He didn't say anything about the fruit. They had an unspoken agreement by this point: don't directly confront the accumulated undone-ness. Not malice. Just exhaustion. A shared understanding that pointing out what *isn't* happening only makes the heavy feeling heavier. He made his coffee and disappeared into the home office, leaving Amelia alone with the slow decay of good intentions.

This wasn't laziness. I need you to understand that. It wasn't even a conscious decision to let the fruit rot. It was something stickier, something harder to name. A resistance that had less to do with *what* needed doing and more to do with the fact that "get healthier" doesn't actually tell you what to *do*.

I know exactly when I first understood this—not because I'm naturally more perceptive than anyone else, but because the moment I figured it out was also the moment I stopped hating myself for procrastinating. I was sitting in my apartment in Chicago, staring at a document I'd titled "Book Ideas." I'd been staring at it for forty-five minutes. The blue light of the screen reflected in the condensation on my lukewarm coffee. The document contained exactly three bullet points, each more vague than the last: "Explore themes of resilience,"

"Consider narrative structure," "Think about audience." I couldn't write a single additional word.

Not because I didn't want to write a book. I desperately wanted to write a book. But "write a book" is like saying "build a house" when you've never held a hammer and you're standing in an empty field with no blueprint, no permits, no foundation, just… grass. Where do you even start? Do you need to dig something first? Pour concrete? For months—literally months—I sat in front of that blank screen, paralyzed not by fear of failing (though that showed up later) but by the sheer impossibility of locating a *first action* within the vastness of "write a book."

It wasn't about motivation. It was about architecture.

The task itself lacked the structural integrity I needed to even begin. So I'd spend hours researching, outlining, reading other people's books, watching interviews with authors—anything *but* actually writing. Which is a perfectly reasonable strategy if your goal is "avoid writing." Less so if you want a manuscript.

That same phenomenon shows up in shared households all the time, doesn't it? The unspoken assumption that *someone* should really sort out the attic. Or *we* should finally get around to updating the family photos. It's everyone's responsibility, which means it's nobody's. A task floating in social limbo, accruing mild resentment with each passing week. Not laziness. An unresolved ambiguity. A quiet friction no one can quite trace back to its source. And it's infuriatingly difficult to address directly because bringing it up feels like nagging.

Now contrast that with a specific request: "Could you carry those three boxes of old baby clothes down to the donation center on your way out tomorrow?"

Suddenly there's an owner. A deadline. And—here's the part that actually matters—a concrete first step. It gets done. Almost effortlessly. Even though hauling dusty boxes is objectively less meaningful than decluttering an entire attic. The difference isn't about wanting to help. It's about the *possibility* of starting.

You might be thinking this sounds simplistic. That I'm reducing complex human behavior to a logistical problem. Fair. And I know what you're probably picturing—some pristine minimalist guru lecturing from a perfectly organized home office while the rest of us struggle with real chaos. (For the record, I'm writing this with three coffee mugs on my desk and a stack of unread books threatening to avalanche onto my keyboard.)

But before you dismiss it as mechanics, try this. Take any vague task you've been avoiding—let's say "organize my finances." Try to start it right now. Exactly as written. What's the first physical action?

Open a spreadsheet? No, wait—which spreadsheet program? Or maybe you should gather your statements first? Which statements? From where? The bank website? Your email? That drawer in the kitchen where you throw mail?

You're already three decisions deep and you haven't actually *done* anything yet.

Now rewrite it: "Log into my bank account and download last month's statement as a PDF."

Notice what happens. The resistance drops. Maybe not to zero—maybe you're still avoiding it for other reasons—but the specific barrier of not-knowing-where-to-start just collapsed. The task went from a foggy cloud of anxiety to a series of concrete clicks you could execute right now if you wanted to.

The research backs this up, though not in the way most productivity advice talks about it. Timothy Pychyl's work on procrastination—the same research we touched on earlier about emotional regulation—reveals something that doesn't get enough attention. Tasks don't just get avoided because they're scary or unpleasant. They also get avoided because they lack clear structure. Because they're *ambiguous*. A task can be completely free of fear and still get reliably stalled simply because it's unclear what actually *doing* it involves.

Think about where that locates the resistance. It's somewhere different than most people look for it. The instinct when you're avoiding a task is to ask yourself, "What's scary about it?" But for a genuinely vague task, that question comes up empty. There's no specific emotional threat you can name. The resistance isn't psychological in the way we usually understand it—it's *structural*. The mind, confronted with an underspecified goal, has to do real cognitive work just to convert it into something actionable. And that conversion work is itself a task. A hidden layer of effort most people never consciously notice they're skipping.

This isn't about lacking motivation. It's about the brain conserving energy. Why expend resources figuring out *how* to start when you can simply… not start? The mind defaults to the path of least resistance. And ambiguity, it turns out, is a surprisingly steep hill to climb.

I watched this play out with a friend of mine—Sarah—over about six months. She'd decided, with real conviction, to "get organized." She bought planners. Color-coded folders. Marie Kondo-ed her closet until it looked like a minimalist art installation. I went over to her apartment one Saturday and it was like the Container Store had exploded. Matching bins everywhere. Labels on everything. A whole

That's the third clue: **responsiveness to standard procrastination fixes.** Emotional avoidance often shifts once the fear is addressed—through reframing, smaller steps, lower stakes. Executive function difficulty persists even after you've tried those things. You make the task smaller, reduce the threat, add motivational incentives, and…still can't start. The techniques built for emotional regulation don't help, because the problem isn't emotional.

Now—these two mechanisms are rarely pure. Most people dealing with chronic initiation difficulty also develop emotional avoidance on top of it, because years of failing at things you're "supposed" to be able to do breeds shame, self-doubt, and eventually a protective instinct to avoid situations where that pattern will repeat. By adulthood, both mechanisms are often running at once, tangled together.

There's a fourth consideration: **unevenness across task types.** Executive function difficulty often shows up most intensely on tasks requiring sustained, self-directed effort with no external structure—long personal projects, open-ended creative work, administrative follow-through nobody's tracking. The same person who can't make themselves write the novel might have zero trouble showing up to scheduled meetings, completing work assignments with clear deadlines, or handling urgent requests from others. That unevenness is informative. A capacity issue tracks structural demands, showing up hardest where external scaffolding is absent. Emotional avoidance tracks *content*—the thing you're afraid of—not structure.

Here's what I wish someone had told me earlier: the cost of getting this wrong is brutal and specific.

detect and therefore harder to fix.

I'll give you a real example from my own work. Last year I had "finish chapter revisions" on my to-do list for three straight weeks. Three weeks. Every day I'd look at it, feel a vague sense of dread, and then do something else. Answer emails. Organize my desk. Refill my coffee for the third time. Anything but the revisions.

Finally, out of frustration, I forced myself to actually articulate what "finish chapter revisions" *meant* in concrete terms.

And here's what I discovered: it meant re-read Chapter 4, mark sections that need tightening, cut approximately 200 words, rewrite the opening paragraph, check all the citations, and send to my editor.

That's at least five separate tasks. Each requiring different cognitive modes—analytical reading versus creative writing versus administrative detail-checking. No wonder my brain kept bouncing off it. I wasn't avoiding one task. I was avoiding an underspecified *cluster* of tasks that I'd have to mentally unpack before I could even start.

Once I broke it down, the resistance evaporated. Not completely—some of those sub-tasks were genuinely difficult—but the initial barrier of "I don't know where to start" just… disappeared. I could open the file and begin re-reading Chapter 4. That's a specific action. My brain knew how to do that.

This extends beyond discrete tasks, though. Consider long-term, open-ended personal goals: "get in better shape," "be more present with family," "learn the instrument properly." These are structurally vague in the same way "clean the garage" is—but they carry an additional layer of difficulty. Even once you've broken them into a specific first action, there's no natural finishing point. The implementation-intention fix has to be applied repeatedly, indefinitely, to keep producing a next concrete step once the last one is done.

That's why these goals are often chronically stalled. It isn't that they're harder to start once. It's that the translation-into-action work has to be redone endlessly.

The psychologist Wendy Wood has studied habit formation for years, and one of her findings is particularly relevant here. Habits form around specific cues paired with specific responses—not around general intentions. A vague goal has no consistent cue built into it, so it can never become automatic, no matter how sincerely you hold it. It lacks the structural foundation for a habit to take root.

"Be healthier" will never become a habit. "After I brush my teeth in the morning, I will do ten push-ups" can. Same underlying goal. Completely different structural integrity.

There's even a connection to the identity-threat pattern we discussed in Chapter 7. A person avoiding a task partly because it's vague and partly because it carries personal stakes will often experience the vagueness as a kind of relief valve. As long as the task remains underspecified, there's no clear moment at which the avoidance has to be confronted directly *as* avoidance. "I don't know where to start" is a more comfortable story than "I'm afraid of what starting will reveal."

I saw this in myself when I kept putting off "learn to draw."

For years I told people I wanted to learn to draw. I bought sketchbooks—nice ones, the kind with heavy paper that feels substantial when you touch it. I watched YouTube tutorials. Saved Pinterest boards full of inspiration. Never drew anything. And I told *system.*

But nothing stuck.

Six weeks later the system had collapsed back into its previous state of chaos. I asked what went wrong and she said, "I just don't know where to begin." Which struck me as strange, given that she'd already *begun*—extensively. But what she meant was: she didn't know where to begin *maintaining* it. "Get organized" isn't a task you complete. It's a state you inhabit. And inhabiting that state requires a thousand tiny, specific actions that her beautiful new system had never actually defined.

The fix? We didn't talk about motivation. Didn't talk about time management techniques or buying better bins. We started with something so small it felt almost insulting: "Spend five minutes clearing off your desk."

That's it. Five minutes. No pressure, no expectation of a complete overhaul. Just a tiny, manageable action with a built-in timer so she'd know when it was over.

And you know what happened? She did it.

And then she did another five minutes the next day. Slowly, incrementally, momentum started building. It wasn't about magically transforming into an organized person overnight. It was about bypassing the initial resistance by making the first step so specific and so *small* that the translation work—figuring out what "organized" meant in practical terms—became automatic. Almost invisible.

Peter Gollwitzer spent decades studying this exact mechanism, though he calls it something different: implementation intentions. The research is elegantly simple. People who form a specific plan in the format "when situation X arises, I will perform response Y" follow through on goals at significantly higher rates than those who simply hold the same goal as a general intention.

Not a little higher. A *lot* higher.

Because the if-then plan does that structural conversion work *in advance*, during a calm planning moment, rather than leaving it to happen live, under pressure. "I will exercise more" is a goal. "When I finish breakfast on Tuesday, I will put on my shoes and walk to the end of the block" is an implementation intention. It removes the ambiguity that would otherwise have to be resolved—from scratch—at the exact moment the task's cue arrives.

And here's where it gets interesting, because there's a subtle interaction with decision fatigue that most people miss. Remember from Chapter 6 how your capacity for self-regulation depletes over the course of a day? A vague task requires an unusually large number of embedded decisions just to *become* actionable. What does "deal with the garage" even mean today? Where do I start? What counts as progress? Each of those unresolved questions draws on that same limited capacity. An already depleted brain is being asked to do more decision-making than a clearer task would require.

Which is why vague tasks are disproportionately likely to be the ones still sitting untouched at the end of a long day.

"Write the report" sounds specific enough, right? But it isn't. Not in the way this chapter means. It doesn't specify the actual next physical action—open the file, review the notes, write an outline, draft the first paragraph. Someone staring at "write the report" on a list is secretly grappling with the same kind of unstructured ambiguity as someone facing "clean the garage." Just dressed up in more professional-sounding language that makes the vagueness harder to myself it was because I didn't know where to start. Which was true, technically.

But once I made the task specific—"spend 15 minutes copying one simple shape from a reference photo"—a different kind of resistance emerged.

Fear.

Fear that I'd be bad at it. Fear that even with practice I'd *still* be bad at it. The vagueness had been hiding that fear, giving it camouflage. As long as the task stayed vague, I never had to confront the real reason I was avoiding it.

So here's the diagnostic question: Once you've rewritten a vague task with a genuinely specific first action, does the resistance actually drop? Or does another excuse immediately appear?

If the resistance persists even against a well-specified step, the vagueness wasn't the primary problem. It was simply a convenient disguise for something deeper—something you'll need to address differently, something we'll talk about more in the next chapter.

But when vagueness *is* the problem—and it often is—what it costs you isn't just undone tasks.

It's a quiet erosion of self-efficacy.

You start to believe you're the kind of person who doesn't follow through. Who lacks discipline. Who can't stick with things. And that belief calcifies over time, layering on top of itself, until it becomes part of your identity. Which is tragic, because the actual problem was never about your capacity or your character. It was about the way you structured the task.

Worthwhile goals get written off as insincere wishes when the real issue was never the sincerity of the wish, but the absence of a concrete first action. The belief that you *could* achieve something slowly erodes under the weight of consistent inaction—not because you lack the capacity, but because you've been systematically setting yourself up to fail by starting with tasks that are structurally impossible to begin.

I'm thinking now of my father, who inherited a small woodworking shop from his own father. A beautiful space, really—high ceilings, good light from the north-facing windows, the smell of cedar and machine oil. But it was crammed with tools and half-finished projects, and over time it became a source of quiet tension in the house.

Every few months he'd announce, with genuine sincerity, that *this* was the weekend he'd finally "get the shop organized."

He'd spend Saturday morning pacing around it, muttering about needing shelves, new paint, better lighting. He'd maybe move a single pile of lumber from one corner to another. Shift a few things on the workbench. Then Sunday would arrive and the shop would still be choked with clutter, and he'd feel… not angry at himself, exactly. Just quietly defeated. As if the shop itself was resisting his good intentions.

It wasn't laziness. He genuinely *wanted* a clean, functional workspace. I could see it in the way he'd stand in the doorway, hands on his hips, staring at the mess with this expression of real longing. Like a man looking at something he'd lost and couldn't quite figure out how to get back.

The problem wasn't motivation. It was that "get the shop organized" is an outcome, not an action. It's a direction, not a step.

I watched him cycle through this pattern for years—literally years—before anyone realized what was happening. That he wasn't failing to *try* hard enough. He was failing to define what *trying* even looked like in concrete terms.

It took my sister—who'd just finished a degree in industrial organization, of all things—suggesting he simply move five tools from the workbench onto a shelf for things to finally shift.

Five tools. A task that took maybe seven minutes.

And suddenly, with that small win under his belt, momentum started building. He didn't organize the entire shop that day. Not even half of it. But he *started.* And starting, as it turns out, is often eighty percent of the battle.

That's not to say specificity solves everything. I remember a client—Maria—who was an architect specializing in historic preservation. Wonderfully talented woman. Perpetually behind schedule on her projects. She'd break them down into incredibly detailed tasks: "research window glazing techniques," "draft preliminary sketches of cornice detailing." But she still found herself consistently falling short of deadlines.

I discovered the issue during one of our sessions when she was describing a particularly frustrating delay on a restoration project.

"I had a *list,*" she said, exasperated. "A very detailed list. Everything broken down into manageable steps."

I asked her to walk me through it.

And that's when I noticed something odd. Every item on the list started with a verb ending in -ing: "researching," "drafting," "reviewing," "coordinating."

It sounded productive. But it wasn't. It was just a catalog of ongoing processes disguised as tasks. Each item described an *activity*—something you could *be* doing—but not something you could actually *complete*. "Research window glazing techniques" is never finished. You can research forever. It lacked a clear endpoint. A deliverable.

The fix was brutally simple: rewrite every task to focus on the output, not the process.

Instead of "research window glazing techniques," she started with "write a one-page summary of three viable window glazing options." Instead of "draft preliminary sketches," she began with "create two sketch variations for the front door cornice."

Suddenly her list went from feeling endless to feeling… doable.

The subtle difference was transformative. It wasn't about willpower or time management. It was about creating tasks that actually *could* be completed. About shifting from a state of perpetual motion—always working *on* something—to a state of actual progress. Having something concrete to show for your efforts.

And the relief she felt, once she realized this, was palpable. She actually laughed. Not a happy laugh—more like the kind of laugh you give when you realize you've been doing something ridiculous for way too long and nobody told you.

It's easy to assume that specificity is about being meticulous. About detailing every possible contingency, accounting for every variable. But it's not. It's about removing ambiguity at the starting gate. About making the first step so obvious and so small that your brain doesn't have a reason to resist.

Think of it like priming a pump. You need a little bit of initial effort to get things flowing, but once the water starts moving, the rest becomes much easier. The hardest part is always that first bit of resistance.

And here's the counterintuitive part—the thing that sounds almost too simple to work but does anyway. Sometimes the most effective way to tackle a massive goal isn't to break it down into smaller pieces at all. Sometimes it's to *ignore* the vastness of the overall objective and focus on creating a ridiculously specific ritual that sets you in motion.

A friend of mine—Ben—was trying to write a novel for years. Plagued by the same paralysis we've been talking about. The sheer scale of the project looming over him like an insurmountable obstacle. He'd tried everything: outlining, character sketches, writing sprints, accountability partners. Nothing worked.

Then he stumbled upon a quirky little habit borrowed from a jazz musician he admired. Every morning, regardless of how tired or uninspired he felt, he would open his laptop and write exactly one sentence.

One sentence. That was it.

No pressure to be brilliant. No expectation of crafting a masterpiece. Just one sentence. Could be terrible. Could be a throwaway description of the weather. Didn't matter. As long as he wrote *something*, the ritual was complete.

And you know what happened?

Most mornings, he didn't stop at one sentence.

Because the resistance to writing wasn't actually about the *writing*. It was about the decision to start. The moment he removed that decision—by making the requirement so absurdly small—the inertia broke. He'd write one sentence, and then another, and then a paragraph, and before he knew it he'd been writing for twenty minutes.

Not every day. Some days he really did just write one sentence and close the laptop. But the cumulative effect over weeks and months was astonishing. He finished a complete draft in eight months. Not because he suddenly became more disciplined or found more time. Because he made starting *inevitable* by making it *trivial*.

There's a lesson in that about the nature of resistance itself. We tend to think of it as a wall. Something solid you have to push through or climb over. But it's more like a threshold. A moment of friction right at the beginning. Once you're past that moment, once you're actually *in motion*, the resistance often dissipates.

The problem is that most of us are trying to vault over the wall when all we really need to do is open the door.

I think about this a lot when people talk about "motivation." As if motivation is some kind of fuel you need to fill up on before you can start. But motivation doesn't work that way. Motivation is usually the *result* of starting, not the prerequisite. You start small, you make a little progress, and that progress generates the motivation to keep going.

The mistake is waiting to *feel* motivated before you begin.